# Images of Industry

## North Pennine Lead Miners in the Regency Period

Ian Forbes

ISBN 978 0 9934117 0 0

Published in 2015 by The Friends of the North Pennines, Company Nº 7240526; Charity Nº 1137467.
Designed by Mosaic (Teesdale) Ltd., Middleton-in-Teesdale DL12 0RP.
Printed by Elanders, New York Business Park, North Tyneside NE27 0QG.

# Introduction

On 24th October 1985 the Science Museum Library (now the Science and Society Picture Library) acquired at auction[1] a collection of lead mining pictures drawn and painted in the early nineteenth century. The catalogue description read: "42 watercolour also 21 pen and ink sketches of lead mining on Alston Moor, Northumberland, depicting all aspects of the work and the miners' lives: recreation, blasting, boring, grating, buddling, making a bargain, wrestling, drinking, 1 watercolour dated 1813, [early 19th century]".

The collection caused a sensation amongst lead mining historians. Here, for the very first time, we saw depictions of working life in the North Pennines from the time of the Napoleonic wars. We saw sacks of lead ore carried on the backs of ponies and donkeys and could study the details of the saddles, the sacks and the scales used for weighing them. We saw the two-wheeled cart used for carrying pieces of lead which we had known about from documents. We saw all the different stages and processes of lead ore washing, or separation, and we saw life in colour. Not the black and white past of early photographs, with their stiff, formal poses, but miners in brightly coloured jackets and trousers, talking or casually meeting, dogs at heel.

In the years since their acquisition several of the images have become familiar to a wider audience. They have proved a rich vein to be mined for illustrations in exhibitions, leaflets, websites and on interpretation panels. Yet never, until now, has the whole collection – every single painting, drawing and unfinished sketch – been gathered together for publication in one volume.

Thirty years after the Science Museum Library bought these wonderful illustrations, this book makes them readily available for the first time. Here, made visible, is the life and work of lead miners in the North Pennines during the Regency period.

## An Enigmatic Portfolio

The importance of this collection of watercolours and drawings cannot be doubted. The archivists at the Science Museum Library must be congratulated for seizing the opportunity to buy it for the nation. Yet even now, thirty years on, there are many unanswered questions which add a frustrating layer of mystery.

Who were the artists? More than one style is evident, and more than one hand drew and painted these little scenes. Where are the places depicted in the pictures? There is no doubt that the images portray the North Pennines lead mining area. But where exactly? Are they representative of real places and real people, or idealised and non-specific?

Who put the portfolio together and why? Some of the pictures are numbered and there are two partial indices. Was the compiler one of the artists or someone else altogether? Several pictures have more than one title, in different hands. As bought by the Science Museum Library they were in two stitched volumes. The second volume included sheets cut from the first volume and numbered as part of the first. Were these put together for a private collection, or was the intention to shine a light on the miners and their hidden workplaces in the North Pennines for the benefit of the wider world?

When exactly were the pictures created? Two have dates, one very specific, but otherwise the only clues lie in the watermarks of some of the paper, which only prove the earliest date the sketches could have been made.

Why was the work never completed? A number of the pictures are unfinished and a number show where alterations to the position of figures have been made as the author has worked out the composition. Sometimes the background figures are roughly sketched in but not worked out. See for example pages 115 and 125.

Finally, who sold the collection in 1985, and where had it been in the one hundred and fifty years and more since it was first assembled? Rightly, the auctioneers respected client confidentiality and would not divulge the name of the vendor. It is inevitable that most of these questions will continue to tease and intrigue as definitive answers seem beyond our grasp. Speaking powerfully of the past, the collection stands alone and without context.

Nevertheless, the pictures themselves can be interrogated and perhaps they reveal enough to allow questions to be answered, however tentatively. Some speculative suggestions follow.

## Where do the scenes depict?

The 1985 sale catalogue identified the pictures as depicting scenes on "Alston Moor, Northumberland". Leaving aside the fact that most of Alston Moor lies in Cumbria (previously Cumberland), internal evidence in the pictures points elsewhere. Where might they have been sketched?

The lead mining region of the North Pennines was extensive, with many mines spread across a wide area. In County Durham the industry was centred on the upper reaches of the mighty rivers of the Wear, Tees and Derwent. In Northumberland, the dales of East and West Allendale were important mining centres. In Cumbria there were mines scattered right across Alston Moor, with a particular concentration around the remote village of Nenthead.

Two major businesses came to dominate the North Pennine lead industry in the eighteenth century and right through the nineteenth century. In Weardale and the Allendales the family business founded in the seventeenth century by William Blackett held a near-monopoly position. In the nineteenth century this business was known as W B Lead, and the name is a convenient one to use for the whole period of the family's lead mining operations. At the time of these pictures the W B mines, together with extensive estates and property, had descended through the generations to Diana Beaumont and her husband, Colonel T R Beaumont.

Elsewhere, the London Lead Company, a Quaker business formally constituted as the "Governor and Company For Smelting Down Lead

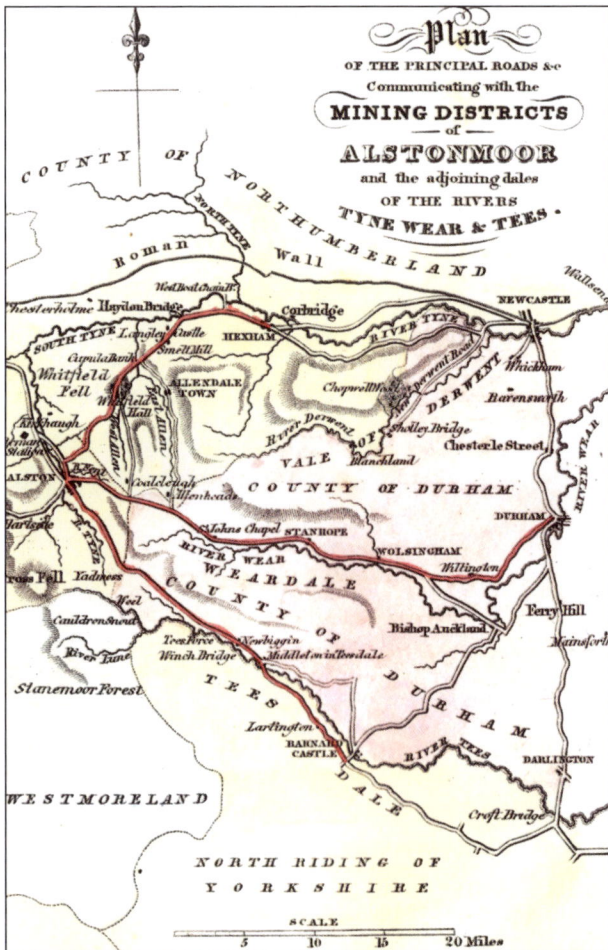

*This early map of the lead mining districts of the North Pennines was published in 1833.*[2]

with Pit Coal and Sea Coal", became the major player in Teesdale and parts of Alston Moor. Despite the powerful presence of these two very large businesses, a number of small mining companies continued to operate in parts of the orefield. Potentially the pictures could have been sketched anywhere within an area of about 1,700 square kilometres.

The hills in the background, particularly those detailed in the horse whim scene (pages 55 and 57), look like a real landscape, but equally do not look like the characteristic long flat tops of the Pennine fells. Perhaps they were painted with artistic licence. In other illustrations where a location is indicated, it is drawn as though the mine or washing-floor is on high land, or open moorland, rather than in a valley where most mines were located (for example on page 77).

However when one studies the pictures and their subject matter it becomes very apparent that the principal artist was primarily interested in people and their work. He or she was not a landscape painter seeing this remote upland as wild and savage scenery in the way Turner was expressing Teesdale at this time. It is difficult to know whether the landscapes in these pictures were drawn or painted merely as a generic backdrop to the scene in the foreground or whether they were taken from life. The former seems more likely. They do not help us locate the working scenes the pictures illustrate.

Yet there are clues within some of the pictures which steer us towards a narrower focus. One painting, of men setting off to work, is entitled 'Monday morning' (page 29). In one of the partial indices it is also called 'From Allendale'. Maybe the picture shows Allendale, or perhaps the men have walked from Allendale and are arriving somewhere else, but the radius must be limited. Here too, though, the scenery and landscape are not entirely characteristic of the valleys and moors of the North Pennines. Was this painted from life, or in the studio?

A drawing of two men fighting is entitled 'The Effects of Alston Brewery' (page 127) but that does not necessarily mean the scene was set in Alston. The Alston brewery supplied a wide area. Perhaps there is a private joke here as well. A number of the agents of the Beaumont mines (W B Lead) held shares in this brewery.

In the picture it is the annual pay day at the mines and money has been spent freely on drink, with predictable consequences. Two men are engaged in bloody fisticuffs outside the public house. Local people must have recognised the scene, the location and the name clearly written on the board above the pub door: 'J Dawson'. The building has been precisely drawn, as though from life, but Mr Dawson's inn is not recognisable today. Why is that? J Dawson himself can be identified from a contemporary directory and parish records. He was Jacob Dawson, and he was the landlord of an inn at Allenheads from at least as early as 1791 until his death in 1827.

Allenheads is perhaps the village in the North Pennines that has changed most over the last two hundred years. In 1845 W B Lead appointed a new chief mining agent, Thomas Sopwith, to manage all its mines. Sopwith insisted a grand house was built for him at Allenheads and he set about transforming the village with new offices, houses, a school and a great deal of investment in the mine and surface works. In short,

*A three-storey public house with a mounting block beside the door, a tree in the foreground, cobbles on the ground and a heather-thatched building to the rear. It is likely that this attention to detail represents a real place (see page 127).*

the Allenheads of the Regency period was unrecognisable a mere thirty years later. The likeliest location of Dawson's inn is the much altered building in the middle of the village known as the old inn and now (2015) housing Allenheads Contemporary Arts and interpretation about the village.

Two further pictures are set in what looks to be a real and particular place. In each (pages 69 and 73) groups of men are meeting mine agents. The view looks downhill towards what appears to be a footbridge leading to a substantial three-storey building. In the background and in front of a stand of trees is a smaller, single-storey building with a distinctive cross or weathervane at the apex of its roof.

*On the left, buildings in the background in 'Stick'; on the right the same buildings in the background of 'Takeing a bargain'. Where are they?*

The configuration of the windows in the nearer building is slightly different in the two pictures: in one there are windows above the door, in the other there are not. Yet the scene is obviously the same in both cases, so some artistic licence has been exercised. This scene is extraordinarily frustrating. Despite the efforts of a number of people, over a number of years, the location, which looks as though it should be so easy to identify, remains uncertain. But there is one place which must be the firm favourite. In each picture groups of miners are meeting mine managers. We can suggest that the scene is likely to have been set in one of only a small number of possible locations.

The Beaumonts (W B Lead) had resident mine managers at Allenheads in East Allendale, Coalcleugh in West Allendale and Newhouse in Weardale. The London Lead Company had managers at Nenthead on Alston Moor and later at Middleton-in-Teesdale as well as at Dufton on the western fringe of the orefield. Yet the buildings depicted in the pictures cannot be recognised today in any of these locations. As we have seen, Allenheads was very significantly remodelled some twenty or thirty years after the drawings were made. Coalcleugh village has almost entirely disappeared. It is probable that the buildings, as drawn, have been altered or no longer exist. The most likely location for the scene is, as with Dawson's inn, Allenheads. Two estate maps show just how much the village was altered in the nineteenth century: the first dates from 1800, the second from 1861 (see page 8).

It is striking how small the village centre was in 1800. The building to the left of the field numbered 10 is probably Dawson's inn. Opposite the inn, across the village green and over the bridge, is the Allenheads

*Allenheads in 1800.*      *Allenheads in 1861.*

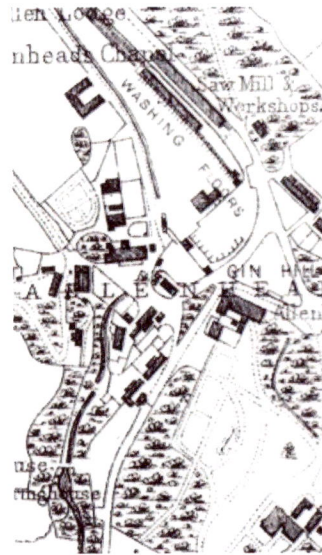

mine agent's house. Today this building is the Allenheads Inn. Is this the three-storey building shown in the pictures?[3] Is the bridge in front of the agent's house on the map the bridge sketched in the picture entitled 'Stick'? Has the distinctive building behind the big house been demolished? This is, of course, all speculation, but Allenheads must be the likeliest location for the two pictures under discussion.

The only picture in the collection with a specific date attached to it is the drawing of 'November 5th 1813' (page 149). As will be demonstrated later, this very lively depiction of drunken abandon illustrates an event connected to the Beaumont family (W B Lead) which entered into local legend as 'The Great Drink'. This scene can only have been set in the W B Lead mining area. It must be in East or West Allendale, or in Weardale.

*A piece of lead on the lead cart inscribed 'W Blackett'.*

The lead cart (see page 143) is carrying a piece of lead clearly inscribed 'W Blackett'. This was the standard identification mark for pieces of lead from the W B Lead mines. Reversed lettering was cast in relief in the bottom of the moulds into which hot molten lead from the smelting hearths was poured. The lettering thus formed a permanent impression in the top of every lead ingot. The name 'W Blackett' is a further clue that the illustrations are associated with the Beaumont mines of the Allendales and Weardale.

Given all the evidence above, none of it conclusive but all leading in the same direction, it is suggested that the lead mining watercolours and drawings show workers employed by W B Lead and illustrate working life in Allendale. It is likely that some of the scenes are set in Allenheads.

## When were the paintings and drawings made?

Because these pictures depict mining and ore separation techniques so wonderfully, it is important to try to date them as accurately as we can. They are a very valuable record of methods, equipment and machinery at a point in time for which pictorial evidence is otherwise largely absent.

Lead mining in the North Pennines enjoyed a completely unprecedented boom during the last quarter of the eighteenth century and the early years of the nineteenth century. Production rocketed, prices and wages were high, and mine owners made extremely handsome profits. The population of the lead dales increased dramatically and new houses were scattered all over the landscape. Yet through this boom period mining methods and ore separation equipment remained much the same as they always had been – basic and labour intensive. They had hardly altered for centuries. There was no technological revolution here in the eighteenth century. Most of the processes depicted in the pictures in this book relied on simple hand tools and locally-made equipment. They would have been utterly familiar to the Elizabethan forebears of the miners shown using them in the early nineteenth century.

Yet new developments were just beginning to come in, particularly on the washing-floors where ore was separated from waste. The hotching tub, shown in a number of pictures (for example on page 93), was unknown at the end of the eighteenth century. Crushing rollers powered by waterwheels, but not shown in this collection, were introduced at the biggest mines in about 1807. Crushing mills were erected at Allenheads and Coalcleugh in that year. The round buddle, ubiquitous later in the nineteenth century, would shortly make its appearance. These images depict the washing-floor at the very beginning of a process of mechanisation which would gather pace as the nineteenth century progressed. What can we deduce about when they were made?

About half the sheets have watermarks. Those with watermarks are dated 1805, so this is the earliest possible date for many of the pictures. The drawings, as bought by the Science Museum Library, were in two stitched volumes including a blank bifolium (sheet of paper) watermarked 1825, so this is the date of compilation and therefore the latest possible date for the drawings. The drawings and paintings were made sometime in the two decades between 1805 and 1825.

The date of November 5th 1813 on one of the pictures has already been noted. However it is also worth noting that this illustration was drawn on paper with a watermark of 1805, so it should not be assumed that the artist(s) used the paper as soon as they acquired it.

The only other dated picture is a scene of the washing-floor, or ore separation area, on a wet day (on page 97). Here, the figure '1819' is unobtrusive in the foreground of the sketch. The paper is not watermarked.

One illustration is entitled 'Stick' (page 73), which suggests it records a confrontation threatening a strike or during a strike. 'Stick' is a dialect term for 'strike'. Strikes were rare in the North Pennines lead mines.

*The date 1819 on the drawing of a washing-floor on a wet day.*

In 1805 there was a threat of a strike in the London Lead Company mines. In 1816 and 1817 there was a strike at these mines, but no details of the events are known. These years just after the end of the Napoleonic wars were extremely hard for lead miners. Demand for lead was very low but at the same time food prices were extremely high. Discontent and an ugly mood rippled through the Weardale mines in 1816, and by the following Spring had spread to Allendale. A notice was posted at the mines:

> *Whereas divers ill disposed persons have lately assembled in a riotous manner & attempted to seduce the Workmen at Allenheads Coalcleugh to leave their employment This is to give Notice that any endeavour to seduce the said Workmen to desist from their work will be punished to the utmost severity of the Law & a Reward of Fifty Pounds is hereby offered to any person who will give information of such offence so as the Offender or Offenders may be convicted thereof.*[4]

Finally, by 1818 the hardship and near-starvation in the mining communities had reached such levels that anger boiled over into a full-blown strike in the W B Lead mines in Weardale. Contemporary records indicate that the mood of 1816 and 1817, and the 1818 confrontation in Weardale between miners and agents, were much more serious and threatening to public order than the rather innocuous scene depicted in 'Stick'. So does 'Stick' illustrate an earlier, minor, incident such as the dissatisfaction caused when miners' pay was delayed for three months in 1812? Like so many of the clues in these pictures, 'Stick' is not conclusive evidence of a specific date.

Another picture is entitled 'Conversation rather serious news' and in another hand, in pencil, 'prices lowered'. This indication of lower prices suggests the period of national economic depression which followed the end of the Napoleonic wars. As we have just seen, this depression had an extremely severe impact on the lead mining industry and people of the North Pennines.

Lead miners were paid only annually, and were paid by piecework according to how much ore they had produced. Every month they were advanced a sum of money ('subsistence') against their final pay. In December 1816, in response to the dreadful economic conditions and the slump in lead prices, the subsistence payment made to Beaumont miners was cut from 30 shillings to 20 shillings (£1.50 to £1) per month. Bargain prices, the prices men received for the ore they mined, were also reduced. Perhaps 'Conversation' refers to this time.

We know that the pictures in this collection have to date from between 1805 and 1825. Whatever internal evidence there is, and it is slight, suggests the illustrations are from the second decade of the nineteenth century, and probably from the period between 1812 and 1819.

## What do the pictures depict?

Although a range of activities is depicted in this collection of pictures, the range is quite narrow. The scenes are mainly of lead mining, lead ore washing, lead ore and lead carriage and of stone quarrying. These are not the observations of someone walking the Pennines and sketching what he saw; there is no attempt to show livestock or farming of any sort. Many miners occupied smallholdings where the family kept a cow or two and a few sheep. Nothing of this is drawn or painted. The

illustrations of horses and dogs in this book are skilfully done, so there is no technical reason why the artist(s) could not have successfully drawn local cattle or sheep. Clearly he or she chose not to do so. There is no peat-cutting for fuel, or limeburning for agricultural improvement. There is nothing of houses or domestic life. There are no women. These are illustrations of working men, rather than a rounded portrayal of life in the dales and uplands of the North Pennines. Whoever drew these pictures had a focussed interest in industry rather than in rural life. Furthermore there is an evident interest in people, in individual character and a marked gift for caricature.

*The artists had a gift for drawing people.*

The mine agent, with his bulging waistcoat, buttons undone, handkerchief escaping from his pocket, an outfit topped by the complacent face of a man who has lived comfortably, contrasts starkly with the obsequious poses of the careworn and elderly miners respectfully doffing their hats. These are real people, deftly sketched in a few lines. The main artist of this collection is enthused by characters and actions and the interplay of personalities, and not by long views or wild dramatic landscapes. Romanticism has passed him or her by.

But the artist is also compiling a detailed set of observations about the North Pennines lead mining industry.

This industry can be divided into several distinct phases or processes. These are mining, washing or ore dressing to separate out the mined ore from waste rock and other minerals, and smelting to convert the ore into lead metal. Binding all these activities together was transport or carriage. Carriage comprised not only taking lead ore from the mines to the smelt mills, but also the onward carriage of lead pieces to the wharves on the River Tyne.

The pictures in this book cover all of the above processes in some detail, apart from smelting. Here, there is only one, barely started, sketch. There are a few depictions of miners underground, but they are not the most convincing and suggest that the principal artist either had not spent much time underground or was not particularly interested in depicting the claustrophobic labyrinth of the typical lead mine. Nevertheless there are several very striking and powerful underground images such as that of a miner climbing a ladder (see page 67). More

care is lavished on ore separation and carriage; in these areas the pictures are a superb record of contemporary practice.

The only other roughly contemporary illustrations of ore separation on the washing-floor occur in papers written by James Mulcaster and Westgarth Forster. Mulcaster was a lead smelting agent and his text, written in 1794, is slightly earlier than our illustrations.[4] Forster was a mine agent for W B Lead, and his book, published in 1821, is slightly later than our pictures.[5]

*Mulcaster's illustration of a washing-floor at the end of the eighteenth century.*

In both cases the authors provided drawings for the purpose of explaining the equipment they described in their text. They did not illustrate working life. There are no people, no action. The paintings and drawings in this book bring Mulcaster's buddles and wheelbarrows, and Forster's hotching tubs, vividly alive. They show real people actually working the equipment – carrying the buckets, or kibbles, pushing the barrows, shovelling the heaps of ore and so on.

We can compare the pictures of washing-floors in this book with Mulcaster's and Forster's drawings, noting similarities and differences.

However ore dressing, or washing, is the only area of early nineteenth-century lead mining for which we have other pictures besides those reproduced here. We have not a single illustration, apart from those in this volume, of pack ponies carrying lead ore or lead, and no other depictions from the early nineteenth century of lead miners in the North Pennines. These paintings and drawings are unique and uniquely important.

One area of work is conspicuous by its absence. We can only speculate on the lack of smelting scenes in this collection, which was made at a time when the glowing furnaces of industry were widely regarded as a suitable subject for romantic art. Typical of this interest in heavy industry, although slightly earlier (around 1780) than our pictures, is David Allan's oil painting of the smelt mill at Leadhills in South Lanarkshire (see page 14).

Perhaps our artist was always more interested in people than industrial processes. Wherever people are shown, the scenes are a triumph of characterisation. The carrier struggles to heave a heavy sack of ore onto the back of his pony; the down at heel but crafty looking drover ambles along following his string of ponies; the hale and hearty miners greet each other, dogs at heel. These are real people doing real work. The pictures are priceless.

*Rich characterisation – a group of lead miners.*

*The romance of industry. David Allan's depiction of a smelt mill.* [2]

## The Collection – an unfinished project

This collection of illustrations of working life is both magnificent and frustrating. It is frustrating because its arrangement is so chaotic and full of holes. The great majority of the 67 pictures have titles or captions written in ink. Nearly all of the captions are in the same handwriting; only two – 'Takeing a Bargain' and 'Pitmen' (on pages 69 and 153) – are obviously written by a different person.

However, the person who added the captions to the pictures was not necessarily the artist. Several pages have a faint, probably original, title in yet another different hand. This suggests that the collection may well have been organised and collated and the picture names added in ink some time after they were drawn or painted. An example of this is 'Bank' (page 59), where the original title, in different handwriting, is 'Banking'.

One drawing in pencil and ink with a sepia wash is titled 'Ore Cart', but in fact shows a cart carrying pieces of smelted lead rather than ore (page 143). It has a pencil scribble towards the top. The scribble reads 'This revers'd'. The lead ingot is carefully copied from life and includes the lettering 'W Blackett'. To prepare a printer's block or etcher's plate from this image would require the picture to be reversed so the letters would read correctly on the print. Do these two simple words suggest that the pictures were intended for reproduction and publication?

Some pictures, for example that on page 71, have more than one caption. 'Conversation' is subtitled 'rather serious news' and in pencil, 'prices lowered'. Perhaps the person who assembled the portfolio of pictures was struggling to find the right words to ensure that the viewer or reader would clearly understand the reason for the evident despondency of this group of men.

As well as being captioned, some pictures are numbered. Twenty-eight of the pictures (including three very incomplete drawings) are numbered in the top right-hand corner, suggesting the collector or compiler intended the pictures to form a sequence. However the numbers on the surviving illustrations do not now form a full sequence. There are gaps in the numbering.

There are two partial indices accompanying the illustrations, but neither includes all the pictures in the collection. The indices are each in different handwriting, with the ink script of the more substantial one corresponding in style to the inked captions and numbers on the pictures.

The more complete index lists 35 pictures and puts page numbers against 34 of them, as though the compiler was preparing a bound volume or publication. Two more picture names and page numbers are added in pencil at the end of the list. The index is not complete; it does not give an unbroken run of numbers. The page numbers listed are 1–8, 12, 13, 15–18, 22–27, 29, 30, 35, 37, 39–41, 43–47 and 49–52. Why are so many numbers missing? Are the corresponding pictures now lost or were they never made? One of the pictures named in the index, 'Poaching', is unfortunately now missing from the collection.

With the exception of 'Poaching', all the pictures listed in the index can be identified in the collection. Where the pictures themselves are numbered, the numbers, with one exception, correspond to the page numbers in the index. The exception is that two pictures have the number 4. On one of them the numeral is written in a different hand, as though it is from a different series.

Some of the pictures which are listed and given numbers in the index are not themselves inscribed with a number. These can mostly be identified by their titles, as the titles on the pictures correspond with the titles in the index. A further ten pictures are numbered in the top right-hand corner but do not appear in the index.

The highest page number in the index is 52, and of the total of 28 individually numbered pictures the highest number is 57. This is inked onto the very incomplete pencil drawing called 'On the Tyne' (page 157). Thus we can conclude that the person who gathered, named and numbered the pictures must have planned to put together a collection of at least 57 different images as a numbered series.

The partial and chaotic nature of both the indexing and of the numbering shows the job was never completed. Either it was consciously abandoned or the author was unable for some unknown reason to finish the work. The highest surviving number (57) is inscribed on one of the least finished drawings, a scene on the River Tyne. The wharves on the Tyne were the end of the journey for the lead pieces whose genesis was as ore hacked from the veins under the North Pennines. Was this collection intended to be a complete record of the process of producing lead, from mining veins of ore to stockpiling lead ingots for sale on the banks of the River Tyne?

However, and problematically, neither the illustrations as numbered, nor the index as arranged, gives us a sequential or coherent story of the lead industry. For example, picture number five shows sacks being filled with clean and washed ore ready for carriage to the smelt mill, and picture number six shows dirty ore being barrowed to the buddle to be washed. There is no logic apparent in the numbering. For the purposes of this book the original numbering system has been entirely ignored as it appeared to make little sense. Instead, the pictures have been re-ordered to give the collection narrative shape.

The order in which the pictures are published here roughly follows the processes of lead production. Illustrations of mining come first, followed by ore separation or washing, and then carriage of lead ore and lead. A number of the pictures are not concerned directly with the lead industry but show people at work or leisure. There are several illustrations of stone quarrying. Stone was of course used in the lead industry, not just for building, but for lining tunnels and shafts. There are depictions of men talking, wrestling or just stopping for a bite to eat. The pictures vividly animate not just the work of lead miners during the Regency period, but some of their social and cultural life too.

It is striking what a range of styles and degrees of completion this collection of pictures contains. It was not only the collation and indexing that was never carried through. This is not a portfolio of finished work. The series of drawings and paintings, like the collation, was either a project in progress or work abandoned. Some minor sketches are drawn on the back of other works, whilst a significant number of pictures are unfinished.

Several different painting and drawing techniques are employed, including watercolour, colour wash, pencil and ink. Some very effective illustrations are almost monochrome with a very limited palette. An excellent example of this style is the jack roll on page 61. Other illustrations are vibrant with colour. The majority are vignettes rather than fully framed scenes.

However, even in the unfinished works, the care and attention to detail is quite remarkable. There is absolutely nothing slapdash or careless in the drawing.

*Attention to costume detail: a button missing off the shirt; the blue jacket buttonholes all carefully delineated.*

Also inserted into the collection is an odd item which seems almost accidentally included. It is a section of a piece of ore separation apparatus and a lengthy manuscript description of how it would work. The manuscript is headed 'On the Washing of Lead Ore'. The author describes collecting samples of ore and minerals from the washers on the washing-floor, establishing their specific gravity and then designing an apparatus using water pressure to effect gravity separation in a closed barrel. As far as is known, such a piece of machinery was never made. The author clearly understood the principles behind ore separation, but perhaps was less sure of the practicalities of life on the washing-floor. However his ingenious machine (see page 159) is moving beyond the newly-adopted hotching tub towards the later idea of the more efficient jig, where water was made to pulse up and down through a stationary bed of ore. The description and the drawing are both unsigned, so the forward-looking design remains anonymous.

What has been preserved and handed down to us in these two stitched volumes is unfinished work. It is superb, high-quality, endlessly fascinating and evocative, but not completed. Was this intended for publication? For the amusement of a circle of friends? A whim, a fancy of an artist and never intended to be seen? We shall probably never know the intention behind this project or the reason for laying it to one side.

## Who was the artist?

This is the biggest and most tantalising question of all. The pictures clearly demonstrate considerable, if sometimes raw, talent. A few are initialled. What can the signatures tell us? There are at least two different artists represented in the collection. Much the slightest contribution comes from the artist who signs himself J B. Three preliminary pencil sketches of figures have been signed with the initials J B, but on one of them the monogram has been added in ink and is not in the same hand.

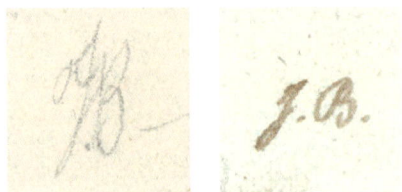

*Initials of the unidentified artist J B.*

A fourth sketch, of a workman (page 91), seems to be in the same style, so may also be by J B. In each case J B's sketches are of figures in action. The artist is using pencil sketches as cartoons in the same way a trained artist would to work out the pose of the main figure or figures of the composition. Only one of these preliminary sketches has been worked into a completed watercolour (page 131). Although the finished picture is not signed, this must also be the work of J B. It is in a noticeably different style from others in the collection. To date, the identity of J B remains unknown, although a suggestion is made below.

Two of the illustrations are signed 'T C' (pages 55 and 105), whilst a further two pictures include the initials 'J C'. We shall return to these initials shortly.

*The initials 'T C' on two of the pictures.*

*The initials 'J C – hidden on the blinkers of the horse (page 143). Is the brand J C on a horse in another pciture also a hidden signature? (page 135).*

The inventory of the pictures drawn up by the Science Museum Library identifies a further possible pencil signature (H P or H D) on the illustration 'Waggon'.

This is probably not a set of initials at all, but a representation of the pin and loop clasp device used to keep the trapdoor on the underside of the waggon closed, initially sketched on the illustration but then not fully worked-up in the final version.

*Waggon – a possible signature? (page 47).*

*Capturing a real person at work (page 47).*

Frustratingly, the great majority of the drawings and watercolours, both those finished and those not completed, carry neither signature nor monogram. We can see from their style that the majority of the pictures are by one artist. Who was this person? The main artist of the collection must have been active in the second decade of the nineteenth century. The artist must have been familiar with, and had access to, the mines and washing-floors of W B Lead (the Beaumonts), with apparently much more limited access to the smelt mills. He or she appears not to have had either the time or the inclination to finish what they started. This person was not just a skilled watercolourist but a gifted caricaturist who enjoyed capturing the essence of individuals with a few deft pen strokes.

There is an evident talent displayed in expressing the human figure and individual faces, but also in animal drawing as well. But this is not someone interested in exploring the fashionable idea of romantic landscape. Landscapes, where they are present at all, are backdrops to the vignettes of human drama and work expressed in the foreground.

Where does that lead us? I suggest there is one person who must be considered the prime candidate for authorship of most of the collection. To identify this person we must examine a remarkable and little-known family who dominated W B Lead before, during and after the Regency period. We start with the father, a man called Thomas Crawhall.

Thomas Crawhall (1748 –1812) was a lead mining agent for W B Lead for the whole of his working life. He was chief mine agent at Coalcleugh mines at the head of the West Allen for twenty years, and then chief mine agent at the Allenheads mine complex for nearly seventeen years.

*Miners' dogs: evidence of ability to draw animals as well as people (page 31).*

He died at Allenheads, still in harness, at the age of 64 in 1812. Thomas Crawhall was not only a respected and successful mine agent: he founded a dynasty of mine agents. He and his wife had a large family and the sons followed in their father's footsteps. They went on to establish an extraordinary grip on the management of the vast and sprawling W B Lead business.

The oldest son George Crawhall (1780 –1852) started his management career at Allenheads under his father. He was promoted to the post of chief mine agent for the Weardale mines, where he served between 1802 and 1813, before taking up a similar position at Coalcleugh for the next four years. He returned to Weardale to take up his old position as chief agent in 1817. Here he served for twenty-eight years until his retirement in 1845.

His younger brother William (1784 – 1849) had an equally long career. He served under his father at Allenheads between 1802 and 1812 and, after his father's death, took over his post as chief agent. He remained chief agent at Allenheads for a further thirty-three years, until ill health forced his retirement in 1845.

Isaac Crawhall (1795 – 1877), a decade younger than William, worked in the Allenheads lead mine office as clerk from at least 1812 until 1822, when he became second-in-command to his brother George in Weardale. He remained at this post until George's retirement in 1845, briefly assuming the head agency in Weardale until he resigned in 1846.

A fourth brother, Thomas Crawhall (c.1779 – 1833), left the North Pennine lead dales as a very young man to work in W B Lead's head office in Newcastle, where he eventually rose to be head cashier. They were a remarkable set of siblings, hugely influential and respected in their chosen fields during their lifetime but little remembered today.

Only one brother, Joseph Crawhall (1793 – 1853), went his own way rather than pursuing a career in mine management with W B Lead. Joseph was apprenticed to a rope-maker in Newcastle. Having learnt the trade he set up his own rope-making business. He very rapidly prospered and Crawhall's factory, on the eastern edge of the booming town of Newcastle-upon-Tyne, became one of the biggest rope-making works in the region.

Commercial success led Joseph into public life and he served on many committees and the town council of Newcastle, becoming mayor in 1849. Joseph Crawhall was a man who enjoyed life to the full, a man with a wide range of interests and a quirky sense of humour. The prominent chimney at his rope works, with its twisted rope motif circling up the column, was a much-loved landmark for generations of sailors coming home up the river Tyne.

But, even though he was running his own business and settled in Newcastle, Joseph kept in close contact with his brothers and they had many interests in common. One above all bound them together. All the Crawhall brothers enjoyed shooting and country sports and met regularly for shooting parties, coupled with gargantuan feasts, with friends on the moors of Weardale and Allendale. They called themselves the Gorcock Club, or the Park House Club. Joseph never lost touch with his roots in the dales and, as we shall see, celebrated this shared life of shooting and feasting in his own joyous way.

Joseph Crawhall's rope-works is long gone but his name lives on and not just in Crawhall Road near to where his works once stood. His son Joseph inherited his father's quirky nature and, as a man of independent means, devoted his life to art and book making, publishing books of local lore and legend illustrated with his own very distinctive and highly idiosyncratic wood prints. Joseph Crawhall's work is still well-known today in his native Newcastle. This Joseph also had a son who was a talented artist and who was the third generation to be christened Joseph Crawhall. One of a group of painters called the Glasgow Boys, the third Joseph Crawhall's reputation as a distinctive stylist and painter,

particularly of animals, stands high today.

So what of his grandfather? Joseph the rope-maker also had artistic talent. He was entirely self-taught and was never trained in drawing or painting but he carved out a niche for himself, in his adopted town of Newcastle, as an amateur artist. His particular gift proved to be as a talented caricaturist who demonstrated a brilliant natural ability to capture the essence of his fellow citizens – the men he met and dealt with every day in public life. Sadly, not much of Joseph's work still exists. What does survive dates from the mid-1820s. Two of his pictures from this period can be seen in the library of the Literary and

'Reminiscences Nº1'.

Philosophical Society of Newcastle-upon-Tyne (the Lit. and Phil.). They are charmingly amused and amusing group pen portraits of some of the great and good of the city. The Lit. and Phil. was a great meeting place for Newcastle society, and Joseph Crawhall was a member. The largest work, entitled 'On 'Change', is not completely finished and the artist has developed the composition whilst making it. In a couple of places Crawhall has crudely stuck fresh scraps of paper over the picture to allow him to overpaint his first efforts. Elsewhere a ghostly dog remains outlined but not fully realised. The second group portrait in the Lit. and Phil., a smaller study of a group of men standing and chatting, is called 'Reminiscences Nº1'.

A cartoon by Joseph, in the form of a print, also survives. Its subject is the famous and bitterly fought election of 1826 in Northumberland. The candidates in this election are depicted in 'Northumberland Races 1826 County Plate Heat 1st' as jockeys in a race. In Crawhall's print, presumably produced to support the campaign of T W Beaumont, Beaumont canters to an easy win over his rivals cheered on by his supporters, who include Joseph's brother, William Crawhall. In fact, Beaumont lost the election, having expended an eye-watering amount of money on the voters to no avail. The style of the print is cartoon-like, and slightly crude, perhaps because of the restrictions of the reproduction process.

Joseph Crawhall had the potential to be more than just a scribbler. A rather fine head and shoulders portrait he painted of his fellow artist John Wilson Carmichael is in the national collection of the National Portrait Gallery. Marshall Hall, in his definitive 'Artists of Northumberland' (third edition 2005), devoted several paragraphs to Joseph Crawhall. Hall described him thus: "Amateur landscape, figure, and animal painter in oil and watercolour: caricaturist: lithographer; etcher; wood engraver".

Marshall Hall continued: "Before becoming deeply involved in his business affairs Crawhall had taken a considerable interest in painting and drawing". Indeed Joseph Crawhall frustrated his friend, the wood engraver Thomas Bewick, because he put his energy into his factory rather than into his art. Hall records that Bewick remarked: "Joseph… excelled as a painter, for which nature had furnished him with the requisite innate powers – but in this he was taken off by his business of a ropemaker". [6]

Although he may have been 'taken off by business', Crawhall retained his interest in art and creative talent in Newcastle. The Northumberland Institution for the Promotion of Fine Arts was the creation of local artist Thomas Miles Richardson. Serving on the founding committee with Joseph Crawhall were the architect John Dobson and wood-engraver Thomas Bewick, as well as other local businessmen and amateur artists. Crawhall was competent enough to exhibit his work at the Institution's first exhibition in 1822.

Joseph Crawhall was a restless soul, always keen to try new ideas. He was particularly taken with the possibilities for print making opened up by the invention of lithography. Lithography was developed by a German, Alois Senefelder, at the end of the eighteenth century, and came to England around 1820. Family tradition had it that Crawhall

*'Northumberland Races 1826 County Plate Heat 1ˢᵗ'*

received lessons in lithography from Senefelder himself. Whether this was so or not, he set up a printing press of his own and dabbled in the process.

In 1827 Joseph Crawhall wrote and printed, almost certainly for circulation only around the circle of family and friends with whom he went shooting, a highly idiosyncratic book: 'Grouse Shooting Made Quite Easy to Every Capacity'. Perhaps the word 'book' gives the wrong impression, for this was more of a collection of pages or plates. It seems likely that Joseph Crawhall produced only about twenty copies, and they were probably all slightly different.

Joseph used his own lithographic printing press to see through the production of 'Grouse Shooting' from conception to finished article.

The tone is set from the beginning. Joseph Crawhall's own name is not mentioned anywhere in the book. Instead, he invents not just a pseudonym for the author, but a character – Jeffrey Gorcock. 'Gorcock' is the old dialect name for the red grouse and would have been a familiar term to all his readers. A 'self-portrait' of Gorcock adorns the first page of the book. He is an old man with bald head, flowing grey locks of hair below his bald crown and a wizened look. He signs 'Jeffrey Gorcock' in a shaky hand under the portrait and claims to be 83. In 1827 Joseph Crawhall was a vigorous 34-year-old businessman and undoubtedly looked nothing like this portrait. What follows is a series of rather crudely drawn cartoons illustrating amusing incidents out on the moors whilst shooting.

The limitations of lithography at the time, with the drawing being made directly onto the stone, probably made sophisticated work difficult or impossible. 'Grouse Shooting Made Quite Easy' was reprinted as a limited edition publication by David Grayling in 1998. Pencil notes on Mr Grayling's copy of 'Grouse Shooting Made Quite Easy', made by Joseph Crawhall's son, show that the author included likenesses of himself (Crawhall rather than Gorcock) in some of the plates, and friends, business colleagues and relatives in others.

Joseph Crawhall had artistic talent, untrained but of a high order. He was intimately connected to and familiar with the lead mining dales. He had a caricaturist's eye for people. He had a sporadic interest in printing and publishing, but rather as an exploration of technique than as a way of producing work for mass circulation.

Was Joseph Crawhall, a young artist with family connections in the lead mining area, the author of most of the pictures in the two volumes bought by the Science Museum Library and reproduced in this book? Was it his talent for caricature which has brought the scenes and their protagonists so vividly to life? Did he encourage a friend ('J B') to join him in this adventure? Might J B possibly be Joseph Bainbridge, another member of the Gorcock club? Did his brother Thomas ('T C') chip-in with a couple of pictures? Did Joseph intend to publish, for the amusement of a small circle, a book of lead mining scenes, much as he did for grouse shooting, but as engravings rather than the more technically limited lithograph images? Did he never quite get round to it? The evidence is not conclusive, and there is a piece of evidence which points away from Joseph Crawhall. This is the handwriting of the two indices in the collection. These lists were clearly each written by a different person. But neither hand appears to be Joseph's, some of whose later account books survive in Newcastle City Library. However in all other respects – as an accomplished amateur artist and whimsical caricaturist with links and access to the lead mines – Joseph Crawhall fits the profile of the author of these pictures very well.

*Joseph Crawhall initialed his picture 'Reminiscences Nº1. Compare with the initials on the horse blinker on page 18.*

## The mine agents

Mine agents were the mine managers of their day. They had to be able to solve complex three-dimensional geological problems. They had to ensure their mines were stocked with supplies and equipment. They needed to possess the skills required to manage large numbers of men. Above all they had to understand and judge the condition of each vein in their mines to enable them to offer the right piecework rates to their miners. Theirs was a complex role requiring a great deal of experience. It is not surprising that a managerial class developed, passing skills and knowledge from father to son, as with the Crawhalls. Many mine managers across the North Pennines were related by blood or marriage and Joseph Crawhall would have known most of them socially through his extended family networks.

Can we go so far as to speculate on the identity of a few of the people shown in the pictures? Two of the illustrations are of miners and mine agents (pages 69 and 73). The chief mine agent is very obviously the same person in both pictures. He is affectionately drawn, clutching his waistcoat with his left hand and in each case with a handkerchief escaping from his pocket. If these pictures represent Allenheads, is this person the chief agent there? This man was of course, as we have seen, Thomas Crawhall, the father of the young and talented artist.

Joseph Crawhall's 'Northumberland Plate' print is accompanied in Newcastle City Library by a key which identifies all the individuals portrayed. Amongst those cheering young Beaumont to victory are his agent, Ben Johnson, and Joseph Crawhall's brother, the mine agent William Crawhall.

Ben Johnson was not a mine agent. He was land agent for T W Beaumont, son and heir of Colonel and Diana Beaumont. He was both a business colleague and a friend of the Crawhalls who took part enthusiastically in the feasting and shooting of their Gorcock Club.

Could it be a much younger William Crawhall standing behind his father

*Is this Thomas Crawhall?*

*In this illustration by Joseph Crawhall of two members of the 'Gorcock' or 'Park House' club from 1836, Ben Johnson is on the right, with George Crawhall on the left.*[7]

*Ben Johnson and William Crawhall (third and fourth from left) in Joseph Crawhall's 'Northumberland Plate' cartoon of 1826.*

in the group of mine agents at Allenheads (previous page)? And is Ben Johnson standing on the right?

For Ben Johnson seems to have possessed a strikingly large nose. Joseph Crawhall, in his caricature of Johnson in the 'Northumberland Plate' print and in drawings of him within the pages of 'Grouse Shooting Made Quite Easy', makes the nose the dominant feature on Johnson's face. Did Joseph Crawhall also include Ben Johnson in this group of mine agents as an affectionate tribute to his friend and shooting companion?

*Ben Johnson from 'Grouse Shooting Made Quite Easy'.*[8]

## The Pictures

The sale catalogue of 1985 listed the collection acquired by the Science Museum Library as comprising "42 watercolour also 21 pen and ink sketches". In fact, including all the unfinished and fragmentary sketches on the reverse sides of some of the pictures, there are 67 watercolours and sketches. There are also two rough and incomplete indices and four pages of text about the washing of lead ore. The pictures are not large. The paper on which they are drawn is about 26 cm by 20 cm, or 10 inches by 8 inches. Every image and piece of text is included in this volume. The Science Museum Library (Science and Society Picture Library) catalogue reference number for each image and page of text is included on the relevant page in this volume. Where the picture has been included in the partial index (page 171) this information too is added.

The pictures can be enjoyed on their own, and they repay close attention for details of clothing, work and faces. For those who want a little more background information, each picture is accompanied by a short commentary.

# Monday Morning

It is Monday morning, early. Miners are streaming from their homes and small farms, heading for the mines. They will be away for the whole week. In their wallets – cloth bags slung over one shoulder – they carry food for the week: bread, bacon, oatmeal, perhaps a little cheese. These eight people have nearly arrived at the mine, having walked from Allendale. The horse whimsey, or winding gear above the shaft, can be glimpsed on the hillside above the leading walkers (see also page 97). Seven carry wallets, the old man does not. The two older men wear old-fashioned wide-brimmed hats. One figure is smaller – is he a boy?

He is the only one wearing long trousers. Is the dog going with them? Four men have walking sticks but two of these have been drawn only in outline. Walking sticks were useful in the mine as well as on the surface. Miners could walk into the mines along the railway tracks, steadied by the stick and keeping their clogs mostly out of the water. Wallets are well-known from oral history and contemporary accounts: however this and the painting on the next page are the only known illustrations from the whole of the nineteenth century depicting wallets and walleters. The mine has not been identified.

*Reference number 1985 – 2032 4. Pencil, ink and watercolour.*
*Page number 4 in partial index and called therein 'Monday Morning From Allendale'.*

*Monday Morning*

# How is 'the my Lad

Two men hail each other with the traditional Dales greeting and clasp hands. The younger man is a walleter: wallet full, he is on the way to work. He carries a stick. The other, unshaven, is smoking a clay pipe. Both men have dogs. The dogs are greeting each other too, one a rough-haired sheep-dog, the other a hunting-dog. Many lead miners kept hunting-dogs. Writing a few years after this picture was made, in 1840, Jacob Ralph Featherstone wrote of the Weardale miners: *"Hunting is a favourite pastime, and they keep among themselves large and excellent dogs, far too swift for hares. The general purpose of the Weardale hounds is for the sport of trailing, to which the men are much attached. A hound is as requisite to complete a miner's establishment at one stage of his life as a wife."* [9]

The left-hand man has been sketched in pencil and then redrawn in a different position, presumably to give the picture better balance. A fine little study of men, dogs and costume.

*Reference number 1985 – 2032 16. Pencil, ink and watercolour. Watermark 1805.*

How is the my Lad

# Going to Work

Two men approach the stone-arched mine entrance, or level. One is carrying a lighted candle sheltered in his hand, the other a short-shafted pick. Both seem to have a bundle of hand drills (called jumpers) on their back, although these are indicated only sketchily on the right-hand man. Both also have a few candles tied round their neck and carried on their chests. Both, too, wear the soft headgear seen in other pictures in the collection. In this collection of pictures such headgear is far less common on the surface but, where a hat is worn, it is universal underground. Is this type of hat part of the costume worn underground – the 'grove clothes' of the miner? Waiting at the mine entrance is a horse and tub with the horseman. He wears long trousers rather than the miners' breeches. In the early nineteenth century trousers were beginning to be worn by some working men. The tub is entirely characteristic in shape and design of those used in lead mines, remaining a standard item throughout the nineteenth century. The man holds a long stick. What is its function? Are the two miners going to catch a lift in the tub to their workplace in the mine? Sketched, but unfinished, in the background is a building; likely to be the mineshop or lodging house where the men are living for the week.

*Reference number 1985 – 2032 11. Pencil, ink and wash. Watermark 1805.*
*Page number 12 in partial index.*

Going to Work

# Pick

A miner stands at his workplace underground wielding a pick axe with a much longer shaft than the one seen in the previous picture. He wears a shirt, long trousers and the soft hat seen elsewhere. The narrow vertical vein of ore is clearly visible in the rock face in front of him.

Mineral veins varied hugely in width from a centimetre to a metre or more. Strangely, no candle or any other light is shown, nor is there any sense of enclosed space or of a rock roof above his head.

*Reference number 1985 – 2032 12. Pencil, ink and sepia wash. Watermark 1805.*
*'Pick' and in pencil after title 'Vein'. Page number 13 in partial index and titled 'Pick vein'.*

Pick Man

# Pick

In this watercolour there is more of a sense of working underground, of an enclosed space, dramatically illuminated by the miners' solitary candle. Very often the men stuck their candles to the rock face with a blob of clay, as shown here. As miners generally had to pay for their own candles they used them sparingly. Miners did not work alone but in pairs, as part of a group or 'partnership', commonly comprising four, six or eight men. Here the two pickmen are taking turn and turn about, the second man waiting, watching and smoking his pipe. There was no ban on smoking in lead mines as explosive gases were almost unheard of. Both men are wearing their 'grove clothes' or work gear of shirt, knee-breeches and soft hat. Unlike the previous picture, in this cameo the vein of ore is not shown streaking through the solid rock.

*Reference number 1985 – 2032 33. Pencil, ink and watercolour.*
*Page number 37 in partial index.*

Pick.

# Blasting, boring

This is a more realistic depiction of miners at work than the previous two illustrations. The painting captures powerfully the essence of working life underground. Men spent many hours boring holes in hard rock using only these simple tools: the hammer and drill or jumper. Working in pairs, the men set up a rhythm – strike the head of the jumper, rotate the jumper in the hole to prevent it jamming, strike the head of the jumper, rotate the jumper…endless hitting and turning slowly drilling holes beside the vein. At the end of the day they will put gunpowder into the holes and fire it to blast down the rock. Their work is lit only by two candles stuck to the rock with clay. The vein is exceedingly narrow and the working area seems generously wide – a great deal of worthless rock has been cut away to give them room to swing the hammer. They are both shirtless – it is hot work deep underground. These two men must hope that somewhere ahead of them the vein will widen out into something more promising. This picture is finished, the background is fully coloured-in and there is no sign of alteration or redrawing.

*Reference number 1985 – 2032 21. Pencil, pen and ink with blue and sepia wash.*
*Watermark 1805. Titled 'Blasting boring' and in a lighter hand in pencil 'vein'.*
*Page number 24 in partial index and titled 'Blasting, boring for vein'.*

Blasting.
boring          Vein

# Blasting

This shows the same action of hand-drilling which was well illustrated in the previous picture but here the poses are more awkward and the space more confined. Both men are kneeling as the roof is lower and there is little room to swing the hammer. Although the picture is entitled 'Blasting' the men are still drilling their shot hole in preparation for blasting. As in the previous picture the man holding the jumper wears a hat, his fellow miner is bare-headed. No candles are shown. The drawing is unfinished. To the right a figure sketched in outline is vigorously swinging his hammer to hit an iron wedge driven into the large lump of rock lying on the floor. After a number of blows the rock will break apart and can be taken away.

*Reference number 1985 — 2032 20. Pencil, ink and sepia wash.*
*Page number 23 in partial index and titled 'Blasting do. (viz. 'boring for vein')*

Blasting

# Boring for Blasting

This is intended to be a group scene underground, but only one figure has been completed. He sits on the floor, holding the jumper vertically between his legs in a firm two-handed grip. His partnership is beginning to sink a vertical shaft down through the floor. This miner wears knee-breeches and the usual soft brimless hat. Lightly sketched behind him his fellow miner is swinging the hammer, or mell, to hit the jumper. Hit, turn, hit, turn. Another faint figure may be an alternative position for the figure with the hammer. The surrounding rock is barely indicated with a few provisional lines. The simple tools of pick, jumper and hammer remained the only weapons in the miner's armoury throughout the nineteenth century and were still used into the twentieth century in small mines. Mechanisation, through the introduction of the compressed-air drill, came very late to lead mining.

*Reference number 1985 — 2032 47. Pencil, pen and line. Watermark 1805. 'Boring for Blasting' and in addition in a fainter hand 'Sinking' Page number 52 in partial catalogue where it is entitled 'Boring for blasting'.*

Sinking Boring for Blasting

# Untitled

Outline from ink of the figure in the previous illustration, 'Boring for Blasting'. The figure is the same, but reversed. It is not known why there are two versions of the same scene on different pages. This drawing is on the back of another ink sketch called 'Dinner' which shows through the paper (see page 115).

*Reference number 1985 – 2032 46 verso.*

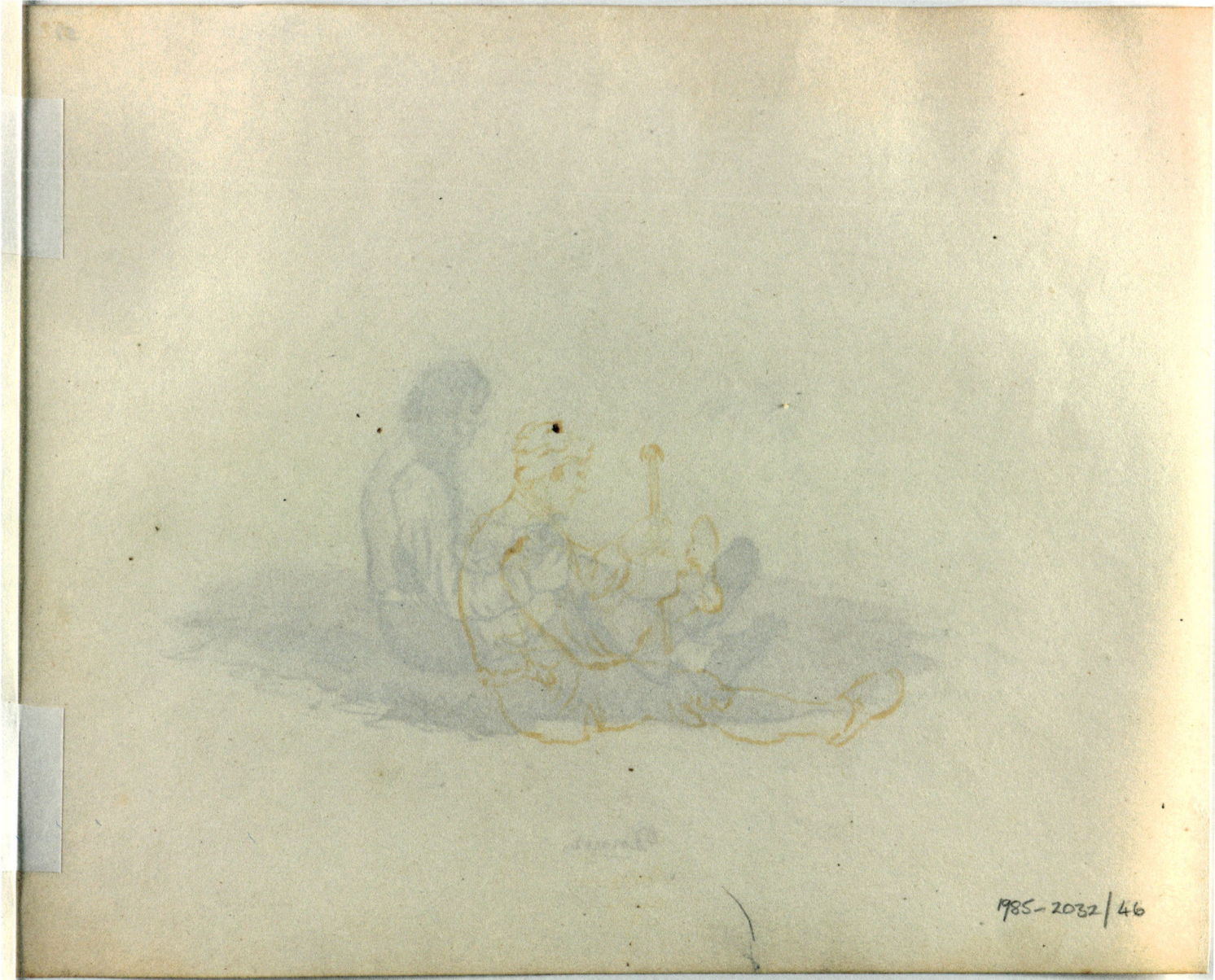

# Waggon

We would expect this scene to be underground, although the background gives no indication of darkness or an enclosed space. A miner working fifty years after the drawing was made would have pushed a similar tub. The size, shape and design of the underground mine waggon, or tub, remained pretty much unchanged through the nineteenth century in North Pennine lead mines. The main change was the replacement of boarded wooden sides with panels of sheet iron or steel. The tub framework continued to be made of wood, as here. In this picture the miner strains, leg muscles bulging with the effort, to push his full tub to where it can join a line or 'shift' of tubs. Then the whole shift will be hauled by a pony along the main haulage tunnel, or level, and out of the mine. The eyes for attaching links to couple this miner's tub to others in the shift can be seen. Once outside, mine tubs were pushed on rails over the bouse teems, or storage bays. Then a trapdoor on the bottom of each tub was opened to let the ore (called bouse) fall through into the teems. Some sorting of the ore had been done by the miners underground but these tubs still contained a great proportion of worthless material. The lead ore had to be separated from the waste or 'gangue' on the washing-floor outside the mine. This illustration, like many in the collection, is very precisely crafted. The miner's clothing is lovingly detailed, to the extent that we can see he is wearing clogs fastened with a clasp or buckle rather than laces. The wheels are cast iron, and here too there is close attention to detail. The characteristic square holes at the centre of the wheels, to receive the axle, are clearly indicated. Wooden wedges were driven between wheel and axle to tighten one on to the other.

*Reference number 1985 – 2032 15. Pencil, ink and sepia wash. 'Waggon'. Title appears inscribed in pencil, then erased, ink title overwritten. Numbered page 18 in partial index and titled 'Waggon' Although the Science Museum catalogue suggests that the initials HP [orHD?] are pencilled on the side of the waggon chassis it seems more likely that this is in fact the catch mechanism for the trapdoor – a detail not inked-in when the drawing was finalised.*

Waggon

# Untitled

A very perky-looking pony pulls one tub of ore. It is a good-looking animal, blinkered and with cropped tail, nicely drawn. Generally the detail here is not so fine as in the previous picture; the sketch is more impressionistic. For example, the flanges to keep the tub wheels on the track are not shown, and it is unlikely that any tub wheels had only four spokes. There is a suggestion that the chains have been shown attached incorrectly on the tub as eyes for chains, halfway up the tub, have been drawn in later. The bellyband on the horse is not complete, only shown down the side of the horse as far as the chain. This picture is unusual in the collection for having no human interest. Who is driving the pony? Reins have been sketched in, but they don't go anywhere. As in the previous picture we have to guess that the scene is below ground as there is no background to help us. Ponies were used to pull tubs from the mine, but usually three or four tubs in a string, rather than just one. By the time photographers came to record underground scenes mine ponies wore a large leather sheet over their back and hind quarters to protect them from wet and sharp rock. Horses were expensive and deserved care and attention.

*Reference number 1985 – 2032 63. Ink and sepia wash. Watermark 1805.*
*This paper is smaller than most, at 19 cm by 19 cm.*

# Vogue

This is a really important illustration as it is the only known depiction of a type of two-wheeled mine tub. A number of mine plans of this era include the name 'vogue level' for a haulage way which was usually not the main roadway out of the mine. Until this illustration appeared, mining historians did not understand the meaning of the term 'vogue level'. The picture, and its title, make it clear that a vogue (the origin of the word is unknown) is a two-wheeled tub running on rails. It is pulled by a man rather than by a pony. The tub is timber with cast iron wheels. It appears to be open-backed, perhaps for ease of emptying, particularly down a shaft. It is an awkward-looking device which seems not to have survived long into the nineteenth century. As this man is neither carrying a light nor wearing a candle on his hat (where miners put candles when they didn't have a free hand), this drawing was perhaps made on the surface. There is just a suggestion in the brush strokes of the watercolouring that the rails on the left of the picture end at the nose of a spoil tip, so perhaps the miner has just emptied the vogue over the end of the tip.

*Reference number 1985 – 2032 14. Pencil, ink and wash. Watermark 1805.*
*Page number 17 in partial index.*

Vogüé

# Filling Out at Shaft foot

Men went to work in lead mines either by walking along nearly-horizontal tunnels, called levels, or by climbing down shafts. Often in the bigger mines it was a combination of both. Lead ore was taken out, for washing, along the same routes: either in horse-drawn tubs along the level, or in buckets, known as kibbles, which were drawn up the shaft. Here, a miner fills a kibble with ore prior to it being wound up the shaft. The size of the kibble, and therefore its considerable weight when full, suggests that this one will be drawn up the shaft by a horse (see the next two illustrations). Miners were paid piecework for the ore they produced, so shovelling broken ore into the kibble was a chore which brought no additional reward. This man wears the usual soft brimless hat and knee-breeches, with shirt and waistcoat. Later, when all miners wore long trousers, they tied them below the knee to maintain the ease of movement breeches gave them. The rock is barely sketched-in but the eye of the shaft, down which daylight comes, is clear in the roof. There is no candle or light shown other than that which floods down the shaft. Many shafts were divided by a wooden partition, with ladders on one side and a haulage way on the other. As there is no ladder here this is purely a drawing shaft rather than an access way for men to ascend or descend into the mine. However it was not unknown for men to go up and down standing in the kibble, swinging perilously from side to side.

*Reference number 1985 – 2032 35. Pencil, ink, grey and sepia wash.*
*Page number 39 in partial index.*

Filling Out at Shaft foot

# Whimsey

This is the first of two almost identical paintings illustrating the horse-powered winder known as a whim, or whimsey, and sometimes simply as a gin, or engine. Whimseys could be put together by the mine carpenter, were simple and effective, and therefore very widely used throughout the orefield. Lead mines did not have either the bulk production or the depth of coal mines, so steam winding-engines remained almost unknown. The horse walks in a circle, turning a drum which has a continuous rope wound round it with the two ends of the rope descending into the shaft from pulleys. There is a kibble at each end of the rope. As the horse turns the drum, one kibble ascends, the other descends the shaft. On deeper shafts the whim was wound by two horses – one at either end of the beam below the drum. A study

on some Yorkshire whimsey shafts estimated that the whimsey typically wound ore up from a depth of 50 to 60 fathoms (approximately 91 to 110 metres)[10]. Note the guide pulleys, known as 'jackanapes', in which the ropes run between the drum and the shaft top. They are suspended from the horizontal beams (the 'jackanapes poles') which brace and tie together the headframe above the shaft and the whim structure itself. At least one man was needed to start and stop the horse at the correct point and to empty the kibbles; his absence from this scene is odd. The background seems very specific, but the profile of the hills is unlike that of most of the rather flatter-topped North Pennine fells. Is this a real place or were the hills painted in the studio? This is one of the few pictures in the collection signed with initials – those of 'T C'.

*Reference number 1985 – 2032 32. Ink and watercolour. Signed in ink: 'TC'.*

Whimsey

# Untitled

This is the same scene as the previous one, with an identical background. The only significant difference in the detail is the omission of the two guide pulleys noted in the previous picture. In neither picture is there a flange or other device to stop the rope from dropping off the drum; it is held in place by friction alone. This picture is neither titled nor signed, nor has it a number in the top corner, so it may be an earlier version of the previous picture. Neither of these two studies has successfully captured the difficult perspective of the horse track as a circle lying flat on the ground. The centre spindle of the whim does not sit in the middle of the circle and the mouth of the shaft also looks awkward. Whimseys, of course, are ephemeral structures but sometimes a flat circular piece of ground near an abandoned shaft shows where a horse once spent many a long hour trudging round and round. At the time these paintings were made, employment of horses for haulage from the WB lead mines was a perk granted to the mine agents who made a handsome income from exploiting this monopoly.

*Reference number 1985 — 2032 56. Pen, ink and watercolour, with pencil. Watermark 1805.*
*Slightly smaller than most at 22.7 cm by 18.6 cm.*

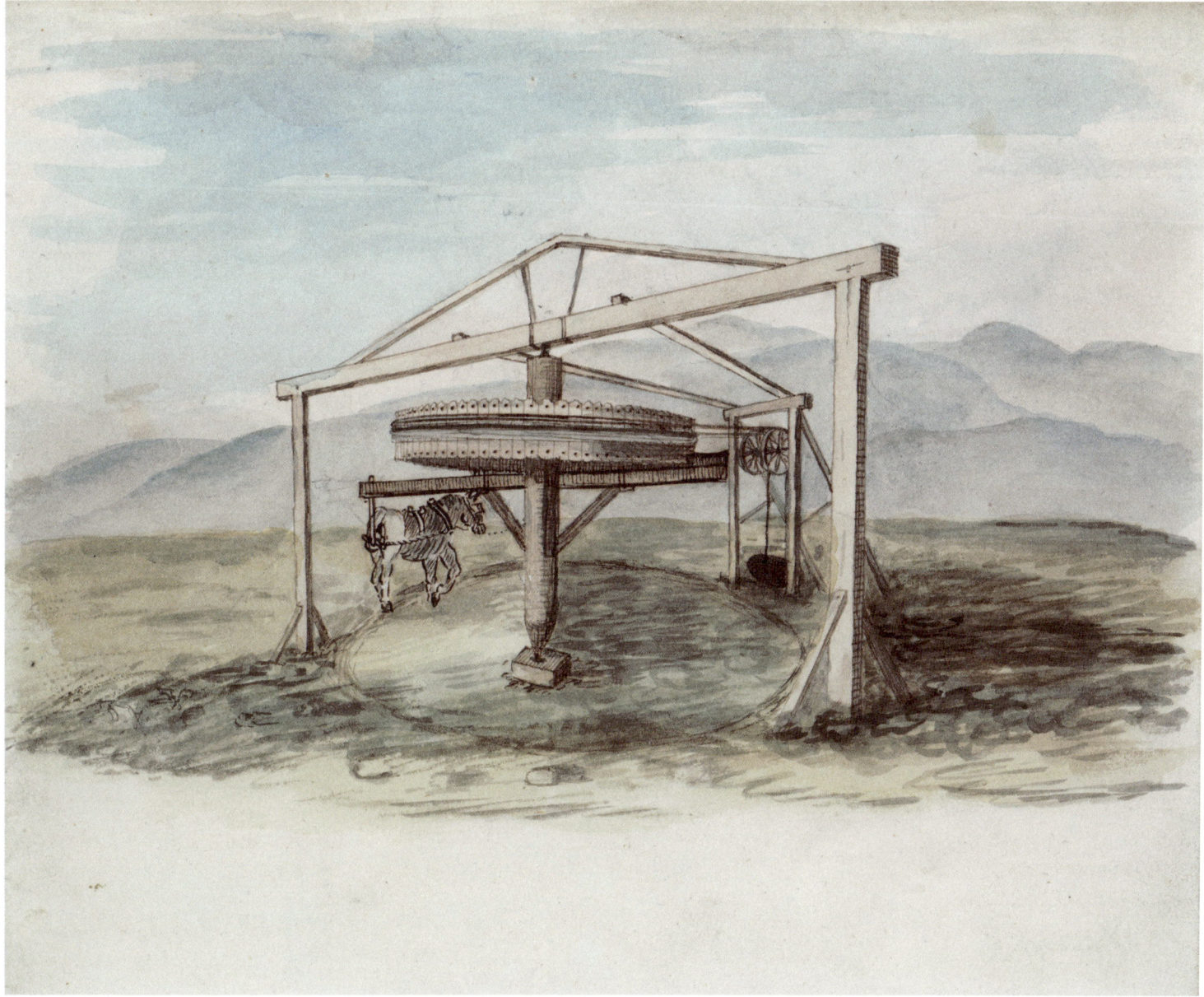

# Bank

The drawing is unfinished but 'bank' is the term for the area at the top of the shaft. It is clear that this picture was going to illustrate emptying of a kibble of ore just drawn up the shaft by the whimsey. The contents are about to be tipped into a wheelbarrow to be taken for processing on the washing-floor. The chain is shown hanging from a sketched pulley wheel above, and then in outline running horizontally towards another pulley, perhaps the guide pulley slung between headframe and whimsey. All this detail has not been fully worked-up in the picture. It is unusual to wind material up the shaft with a chain rather than a rope. The structure against which the man is holding his left hand has not been fully detailed but the man himself has been carefully articulated. The wooden kibble, with its iron bands, and the wheelbarrow constructed entirely of wood and with a wooden wheel, are completely characteristic of the time and place. Indeed wheelbarrows such as this survived unchanged in design right through to the period when photography captured mining scenes towards the end of the nineteenth century. They were made by the mine business's own joiners, in company workshops.

*Reference number 1985 – 2032 45. Pencil, pen and line. 'Bank' replaces an earlier fainter inscription just above it in pencil 'Banking' written in a different hand. Included in the partial index as 'Bank, at' but without a page number allocated to it.*

Bank

# Jack Roller

This is a splendid study of three miners working a piece of equipment universally known in the North Pennines as a jack roll, or jack roller, and on the Derbyshire mines as a stow. Where a shaft was relatively shallow, the power of the horse was not needed to haul the kibbles of ore to the surface; the work could be done instead by man-power using smaller kibbles. The jack roll is of course very similar to the winding gear above a well, and is probably as ancient in origin. Jack rolls were so simple and cheap to make and operate that they lasted at small mines right through until the early twentieth century. The writer remembers talking to an old miner whose early memories of entering his father's mine were of being lowered down the shaft in a kibble by a jack roller.

In this picture it takes two men to wind up the tub of ore whilst the third person is about to grab the handle of the kibble and pull it away from the shaft mouth. The rope is continuous, like the rope on the horse whimsey, so another kibble will be at the bottom of the shaft about to be filled, as in the picture on page 53. The individual character and the costumes of the three miners are magnificently captured. The man on the right is particularly ragged in his grove clothes, with holes in the knees of his breeches and his stockings. It looks as though the buttons are off his breeches at the knee. His waistcoat looks too small for him. He wears the miner's headgear of a soft hat.

*Reference number 1985 – 2032 13. Pencil, ink and russet wash. Watermark 1805.*
*Page number 16 in partial index.*

Jock Roller

# Untitled

A pencil sketch signed by 'JB' is a first study for a jack roller. Numbered 28 and presumably destined for the collection of images which, like this picture, was never finished.

*Reference number 1985 – 2032 25. Pencil. Watermark 1805.*

# Untitled

This atmospheric little vignette is diffused with sombre melancholy. In depicting a young miner (is it a boy?) lighting his way with a candle in a lantern, the artist has given him a downcast expression. His trousers, presumably his working clothes, are worn-through, with massive holes at the knee. Is that a hint of a railway line in front of him?

Is he going to work underground? Thinking about another day turning the handle of a ventilation fan, or opening and closing a ventilation door in near darkness? Coming out of the mine? Walking home in the dark after a long shift on the washing-floor? What is he thinking about? Impossible to know.

*Reference number 1985 – 2032 57. Pen, ink and sepia wash, with blue wash.*
*23.3 cm by 19.2 cm.*

# Untitled

This dramatic picture shows a miner climbing a ladder in the heart of the mine. Even in the deepest mines ladders were the usual way for miners to descend and ascend, sometimes hundreds of feet. A series of ladders in the shaft was punctuated by a series of stagings or platforms. Climbing back out of the mine after a day's shift was hard physical work. As most miners gradually developed lung disease from the dusty atmosphere underground it was only the youngest and fittest men who worked in the deepest parts of the mine. This is one of the most powerful pictures in the collection, with its dramatic dark background and the miner himself strongly illuminated by the circle of light thrown by his candle as he climbs one-handedly. If a miner needed both hands he stuck his candle to his hat with a blob of clay. Ladders might have been hard work but they were an improvement on the earlier stemples. Stemples were merely pieces of wood wedged across the corner of a shaft at appropriate heights for men to climb, stepping from one to the next. Our miner's grove clothes, or working clothes, (grove is the old word for mine) are extremely ragged. His trousers have a large hole in the left leg. The right leg of the trousers ends below the knee. Tied to his back is a bundle of jumpers or miners' drills. He is on the way to work.

*Reference Number 1985 – 2032 59. Ink and sepia wash, with black.*
*Like the previous picture, slightly smaller than most in the collection at 23 cm by 19 cm.*

# Takeing a Bargain

This is an important day in the mining calendar, crucial for the earnings, and therefore the wellbeing, of nearly every family in the neighbourhood. Six men, a partnership of miners, doff their hats to the mine manager or agent who stands before them paunchily, hat resolutely on his head, kerchief dangling from his pocket, stomach bursting out of the undone middle button of his yellow waistcoat. These are real people, surely, drawn from life. Each has his own character: one is old-fashioned enough to be still sporting a wig. There is perhaps some poetic licence in the concept of taking a bargain in this way, out of doors, almost informally. Bargains were the quarterly contracts between groups of miners (usually four to eight, but in this case, six men) and the mine agent. The bargain set the rate of payment for the lead ore raised by the men in the following three-month period, or the rate per fathom of six feet (nearly two metres) if the gang was driving a tunnel or sinking or raising a shaft. Bargain setting, at least as we know it from records from the mid nineteenth century, was an organised and regulated occasion. All the miners were offered bargains on the same day. The following day, those who had refused the initial price or who had for some other reason not been given a contract were offered work. This second day was called 'placing day' and the objective was to ensure full employment at rates that were satisfactory to both mine owners and men. It is therefore unlikely that a bargain would be set in what seems like an out of door chance encounter with no other groups of miners present. The characters are delightful and the costume surprisingly colourful to the modern eye. These miners are not in their grove clothes, but are dressed in respectable coats and breeches. The two closest to the agent, older men, have been the spokespeople for the group. The early nineteenth century was often a troubled time in industry, with crippling food prices, discontent rife amongst workers and real fear of revolutionary contagion spreading from France. But there is no suggestion here of rough, tough men or militancy — the miners are both respectable and deferential. The drawing looks like a real place: the same mine agent and the same buildings are depicted in a further illustration in the series (see page 73). It is not certain where this place is, so for now, the scene remains to some degree enigmatic and tantalising. Is it Allenheads? See the discussion in the Introduction on pages 7 and 8 .

*Reference number 1985 – 2032 31. Pencil, ink and watercolour. Watermark 1805. The Science Museum catalogue has: 'number 35 pencilled to replace corner now repaired (confirmed in index)' The writing of the title is in a different hand to the previous titles. Given page number 35 in the partial index with title 'Takeing a Bargain'.*

Taking a Bargain

# Conversation rather serious news

This is a fine study of a group of five miners, meeting on the street and deep in conversation. Four of the men are finished portraits: surely as in the previous picture they are drawn from life. These are real dalesmen of the early nineteenth century. The artist has enjoyed lavishing great attention on the details of their clothing – every button is carefully picked out. For some reason the fifth man remains unfinished, a ghostly disconsolate outline. The attitude and stance of all the men very well conveys the 'serious news' of the title of this piece – prices for their work have been lowered. There were several periods of poverty and extreme hardship in the lead mining communities during the early nineteenth century. The most serious was in the years following the defeat of Napoleon, when the whole country was gripped by economic depression. 1818 was a particularly bad year. Lead prices had been falling relentlessly for more than a decade. In 1817 lead was selling for half the money it made in 1805. In response to this crisis, the incomes of miners were savagely cut and families faced real hunger. Many men took to poaching to survive, roaming the countryside in gangs. Encounters with militiamen took place in several locations. The authorities remained scared of revolution and cracked down hard on lawlessness, strikes or dissent. One incident of 1818 has become legendary. The 'Battle of Stanhope' took place when some well-known Weardale poachers were arrested and then freed by their fellow miners in a bloody battle with the officers of the law. Does this picture depict 1818 or an earlier, less desperate time? These men hardly look like troublemakers, nor do they look as though they cannot afford to dress in decent clothes. They seem only worried about their jobs, not on the brink of revolt.

*Reference number 1985 – 2032 44. Pencil, pen and line, watercolour. Titled 'Conversation rather serious news' and in another hand in pencil 'prices lowered'. Included as page 49 in the partial index with the title 'Conversation'.*

Conversation, prices lowered
rather serious news

# Stick

On page 69 all was civility as the men agreed their bargain. Now the mood has changed. The place is the same; the same mine agent still nonchalantly holds his lapel. But here he is confronted by a delegated group backed up by a large mob. The miners in this drawing are younger, more aggressive. The agent, too, is no longer alone. He is supported by three other men with a fourth, unfinished, figure a little further back. 'Stick' is a vernacular term for strike: the miners are in demanding mood. Strikes were extremely rare in the lead mining districts. Generally lead miners were not militant, had good relationships with the mine agents and did not combine in unions like the coal miners further east. There was a famous strike against the new agent, the outsider Thomas Sopwith, at Allenheads in 1849 but otherwise the miners only withheld their labour when cornered by the desperation of extreme poverty. This happened when the industry was in fatal decline in the late 1870s and early 1880s and also in the deep post-Napoleonic war depression. In 1818 the miners of Weardale went on strike, but the Allendale miners did not. If this drawing is of the agent at Allenheads, as argued in the Introduction, does this drawing illustrate an incident at Allenheads as yet undiscovered by historians? The mine agents, surely, are real people drawn from life. Are they Thomas Crawhall and his son William? Does William's friend Ben Johnson stand with them? The picture has been much scribbled on, with text now barely legible. One faint scrawl appears to read '*F. preventing*' rather than '*F. printing*' as the catalogue suggests. Is the situation being defused? Is 'F' the artist Joseph Crawhall's father? Once again. time, place and people remain elusively just beyond our grasp.

*Reference number 1985 – 2032 42. Pencil and ink. Watermark 1805. 'Stick' and in ink 'Delegates'. Included in the partial index with page number 47 and the title 'Stick'. The Science Museum Library catalogue says "Inscribed notes in pencil left including initials J B and others, pencil note to right of title, faint possibly 'F. Printing.'*

Delegates

Stick.

# Untitled

The next group of pictures illustrates the second phase of lead mining: the separation of the mined mineral, known as 'bouse', into nearly-pure lead ore and waste material. For centuries before the time of these illustrations, ore washing, as it was known, had been a simple and crude process, highly labour-intensive, and hardly changing over the years. The opening twenty years of the nineteenth century saw the first attempts at mechanisation with new equipment and techniques introduced. These pictures are a valuable record of that time of change for they illustrate both the old and the new. We have a description and an illustration of the eighteenth-century washing-floor in Mulcaster's work (see page 12) and Westgarth Forster described the new and partially-mechanised washing-floor in 1821.[11] Our paintings and drawings were made in the period of modernisation which began between the publications of these two authors. But change was slow and washing, like mining, continued to rely on vast amounts of manual labour. This unfinished study of a boy pushing a wheelbarrow epitomises the sheer hard work the lead industry demanded. It is unclear what is represented in the background, and interesting that this is the only illustration in the collection which shows any wildlife – a flock of birds overhead. The sketch is signed in pencil 'J B'. To date 'J B' has not been identified. J B is also responsible for the pencil drawings on pages 63 and 133.

*Reference number 1985 – 2032 28. Pencil.*

# Filling Buddle, Barrow

This watercolour shows the old way of washing and separating lead ore. From Elizabethan adventurer to early-nineteenth century washermen, every generation knew this scene. Lead ore is heavier than other minerals it is found with, so ore separation was straightforward using gravity and water. A buddle was merely a flat, sloping surface down which a stream of water ran. The washers built a pile of bouse from the mine at the head of the buddle and then turned, raked and shovelled it through the stream of water. Superficial dirt was washed off down the buddle, as was the lighter waste rock and mineral. Heavier lead ore stayed near the top end of the sloping buddle.

Here, two men prepare for buddling, loading their barrows at the large heap of bouse from the mine then wheeling them to the head of the buddle. The buddle in this illustration is not clearly defined; the focus is on the men, the ore and the wheelbarrows. It is all delicately coloured in brown and blues: only the red cheeks of the washer betray the effort required. Unusually he sports what look like braces.

The barrows are of traditional wooden construction, shod with an iron tyre and running on a plank barrow-way. The scene is set on an exposed upland plateau, with a sinuous watercourse supplying water for the buddle. The left-hand stream is the one which will feed the buddle but no sluice mechanisms or water control devices are shown. The headboard at the top end of the buddle is shown, with a notch or depression in the centre over which the water will flow when the buddle is working. Lying across the heap of unwashed ore on the buddle is a colrake, the implement which will be used to rake the bouse through the running water.

*Reference number 1985 – 2032 6. Pencil, ink and watercolour. Watermark 1805.*
*Numbered 6 first in pencil and then in ink.*
*Given page number 6 in the partial index and entitled 'Barrow Filling Buddle'.*

Filling Buddle
Barrow

# Buddleing

In 1794, James Mulcaster, a smelter at Langley Smelt Mill in Northumberland, wrote an account of lead smelting which includes a description of ore washing. These pictures help Mulcaster's text leap into busy life. A unique archive, they paint real people working at tasks Mulcaster describes in words. *"...the* **Buddle**, *which Buddle is only a piece of floor of Wood or stone laid very sloping abt. 6 ft. in length & 2 in breadth, on the one side whereof, a Board of the same length as that side & abt. 8 ins. broad is set on edge & back'd with Earth to the height of itself; this is called the Buddles-Head, as a Gap or indenture cut at equal distances from its two ends for a small stream of Water to pass thro' is called its Eye. This Buddle being charged...the necessary water, which is kept running near at hand for the purpose is turned into it, & a Channel made for it close to the Head-board of the Buddle; which done the Washer, with his Shovel or Coal- rake, begins to make new channels for it across the first, continually pulling or turning over a part of the heap to the side next him with the water running amongst it 'til he has passed in this manner thro' it to the other end, where he turns off such light (being supposed the worthless) parts as the water has driven to the skirts of the Heap, leaving the remainder in a semi-circular form. These Tails (they are called Tails at a Smelt Mill but at the Lead Mines Cuttings), being disposed of by being cast away, he again turns the water into the Buddle, & passes thro' the heap in the same manner as at first, repeating such puttings thro' of the Buddle, with the circumstances of diverting the water from it & discharging a quantity of Tails at every repetition 'til he judges his Work (what is still left in the Buddle) sufficiently dashed, as it is called, meaning made fit for the Tub & Sieve...".*[12]

Here, two men, curiously out of proportion one with another, work the buddle as a team. One turns the bouse in the stream of water with a long-handled shovel, exactly as Mulcaster describes, whilst his companion is kneeling to pick out the lumps of pure ore to put into a kibble. One of the delights of these pictures is that they show details not recorded anywhere else. This painting is a good example. The man with the shovel uses his right leg as a fulcrum whilst working the bouse. To protect his thigh and his clothes a leather guard is strapped to his leg where the shovel handle would otherwise rub. As in other drawings the attention to the costume is wonderful. A tiny detail – the kneeling man has unbuttoned the bottom of his breeches to allow him to kneel freely.

*Reference number 1985 – 2032 1. Pencil, ink and watercolour.*
*The partial index has this as its first picture on page one with the title: 'buddleing shull'.*

Buddling

# Kibble

This unfinished drawing, 'Kibble', demonstrates yet again that lead ore washing was extremely labour intensive. Two men carry a bucket, or kibble, clearly heavily laden. Perhaps it is a bucket of pure ore from the buddle, being taken to the bingstead for storage prior to smelting. This is not a kibble from the drawing shaft as it does not have a loop handle on which to hook a rope. Neither man is young. Both are careworn.

It was not uncommon for older miners, too short of wind to continue working underground, to be given employment on the surface at the washing-floors. Faint pencil lines show that each man was initially intended to be wearing a hat, but now one wears the traditional miners' soft hat and the other goes bare-headed. Behind them an unfinished figure struggles to carry a much larger and heavier lump of rock.

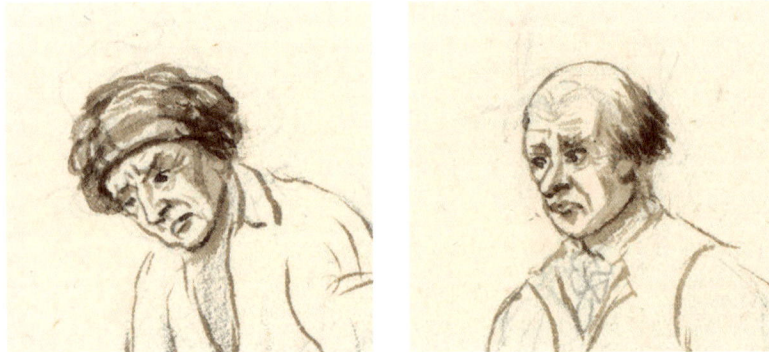

*Reference number 1985 – 2032 22. Pencil, pen and line. Watermark 1805.*
*Allocated page number 25 in the partial index where it is called 'Kibble, carrying'.*

Kibble

# Shaddering and Knocking

*It's early in the morning*
*We rise at five o'clock*
*The little slaves come to the floor*
*To knock, knock, knock.*

And so they did, later in the nineteenth century. This well-known washerboys' song (*Fourpence a Day*) paints a familiar picture of young children – boys – working on the washing-floor and at the knockstone, breaking up ore. Yet these illustrations tell a different story. It is not boys working at the washings, but grown men. Perhaps child labour came later, with mechanisation and consequently with less need for skill. This completed painting illuminates a key feature of the washing-floor – the knockstone. The title of shaddering and knocking refers to the two actions going on here. One washerman sits on the knockstone as he breaks up (shatters or shadders) large pieces of bouse. This is necessary when the galena, or lead ore, is intermixed in the same lump with other minerals. The lump has to be broken up into small fragments before the heavier ore can be separated out. The painter understands this: half of the large lump being smashed is blue (representing galena) and the other half is a dull grey (rock). The shaddering hammer has both a hammer head and a pointed end, which can be used like a pickaxe. In most of these illustrations one cannot be certain whether the miners and washermen are shod in shoes or clogs. From the visible soles of the man shaddering, he at least is wearing clogs, his wooden soles rimmed with clog irons. The second washerman is knocking. He sits on a bench and breaks smaller pieces, perhaps shaddered ore or perhaps ore brought here from the buddle or the grating (see page 89). His flat-faced hammer is a tool particular to ore separation and is called a bucker. Buckers and knockstones continued to be used throughout the nineteenth century and several knockstones still survive in out of the way places in the North Pennine hills. Breaking rocks this way was slow work, and an innovation in the early years of the nineteenth century was the roller crusher. This consisted of two iron rollers revolving against each other and crushing ore which passed between them. The crusher was driven by a waterwheel. It is interesting that no roller crusher is illustrated in this series of pictures. Either the paintings were made before roller crushers were introduced in about 1807, or else the artist was not interested or did not encounter them.

*Reference number 1985 – 2032 2. Pencil, ink and watercolour.*
*In the top right-hand corner a pencilled '2' overwritten '2' in ink.*
*The partial index has the same page number for this picture.*

*Shaddering & Knocking*

# Tubbing

Cold, wet hands chapped red raw through constant immersion in water, back aching from stooping, twisting and shaking the loaded sieve. This is the life of the washerman doing tubbing, finely illustrated here in muted browns. Mulcaster describes the tubbing process:

*"then a Tub is provided, abt. 3 ft. in height & 2½ in Diamr., filled not quite but almost so with Water, and also a Sieve, which is a small wooden Vessel with two Handles & a bottom of wove Wire. Into the Water of the Tub this Sieve, with a charging or loading of about one Gallon of such substance as is to be washed, is immersed nearly up to its brim, where being tossed to & fro' for some time, the minute parts of such substance are sifted thro' & sink in the Tub, whilst at the same time the lightest parts, which from bulk cannot pass that way, are thrown uppermost within the Sieve… which done, it is taken out of the Water and placed upon a Bar of Wood or Iron for a Rest, and laid across the top of the Tub, where, to skim off the light parts, which at this first setting are generaly fit only for the Waste or Cutting Heap, a small Instrument called a Limb is used, being a semicircular piece of Board abt. 8 Ins. long & edged with Iron on the curved side; … at the Mines where there are many Bodies almost as ponderous as Ore, and where that Ore is frequently brangled in with those Bodies, such Settings must be repeated perhaps several times…".*[12]

Here we see it all: the tub, the sieve submerged, the limb, the rests for the limb as well as the bucket, or piggin, to receive the pieces of pure lead ore. And every washing 'repeated perhaps several times'. Such slow work, and more ore arrives all the time, poured from the wheelbarrow.

*Reference number 1985 — 2032 8 Pencil, ink and sepia wash. Watermark 1805.*
*Given the same number — page 8 — in the partial index.*

Tubbing

# Buddleing Rake

Washing seems a simple operation, with unsophisticated and cheap equipment. Yet both judgement and much manual handling are required at every stage. As we have seen, the same material might have to be buddled or tubbed over and over again. Material is carried back and forth between the different parts of the washing-floor. Mixed or 'brangled' pieces picked from the buddles, or brangled pieces of ore in the sieve of the tub, have to be broken down further before the lead ore can be successfully separated. Back to the knockstone they go, then again to the buddle or tub. And then there is the small stuff which falls through the mesh of the sieve. Mulcaster picks up the story: "…*I come now to that part which has pass'd thro' the Sieve, which is called Smithorn or Smiddon, with which at times the Tub will be so filled that the bottom of the Sieve will strike upon it; and when this is observed, the Tub is then emptied of it, and it is carried to the Buddle, where with a less powerful stream of Water it undergoes as many Puttings- thro' in manner as before described, as will make it clean, and when it is so, it is joined to that prepared in the Sieve as being equaly fit for smelting…*".[12] This painting might represent any stage in the buddling process, but the ore here appears to be nearly washed clean. There is not much waste rock still on the buddle; the heap is glistening blue with galena or lead ore. The washer has dropped his shovel (although he is still wearing the protector strapped to his leg) and has turned to using the colrake. By drawing the material carefully through the stream of running water he is able to wash away the lighter waste, leaving the heavier lead ore behind. A wooden piggin, or bucket, stands ready to receive it. The lad doing the raking looks young and the man with the barrow is elderly. A third, incomplete, figure may be holding a sack to fill with clean ore. This scene depicts more of the setting than the previous studies of buddling. It shows that this was a mine of some size for in the background we see the bouse teems or storage bays where ore was stored after being trammed from the mine. A mine tub is sitting on the rail track over one of the teems, and it can be readily understood how the bouse was emptied from the bottom of the tub into the teem. As partnerships of miners were paid only for pure lead ore, not for the impure bouse from the mine, the bouse of each partnership was stored in a single teem until it had gone through cleaning on the washing floor. The feature on the hillside behind and to the right of the mine tub appears on page 111 as well, so is clearly significant, but is as yet unidentified.

*Reference number 1985 – 2032 43. Pencil, ink and watercolour. Watermark 1805.*
*Numbered 48, the same page number given to the picture in the partial index.*

Buddleing.
Acke

# Grateing

This is a finished painting, unusual in this group, with stronger colours than some of the other delicately precise figure studies. The word 'Hotching' is scribbled upside-down in the top right-hand corner of the picture, but this scene does not depict hotching. It shows the recently introduced process of 'grating'. Mulcaster's late eighteenth century-description of ore washing does not mention grating. Yet twenty years after Mulcaster's 1794 text, grating was common practice. In the early nineteenth century mine owners were beginning to appreciate that investment in ore washing, in the washing-floor, made sense. Smelters needed their lead ore to be as pure as possible if they were to make good quality lead and use less fuel. The temptation for the washers was always to cut corners, to be careless and lazy. If they could get away with it they sent ore off to the smelt mills still full of bits of rock and unwanted minerals. Early in the nineteenth century the Beaumonts (W B Lead) tackled the problem head on. They restructured their lead business and introduced posts called 'Inspector of Washing Ore' or washing master. The washing masters' primary task was to ensure quality control at the washing floor. The old man leaning on his stick in this illustration may be a washing master keeping a beady eye on proceedings. Investment was also beginning in equipment as well as in personnel. Buddling required no more than a stream of water and a few planks nailed together to form a flat surface. Grating needed proper structures, as illustrated here. The painting shows a stone platform, a chute down which the bouse pours onto the grating, the iron casting of the grating itself and a piped or boxed water supply rather than a mere stream. The mouth of the wooden box bringing water to the grating can clearly be seen. All this investment was necessary once hotching tubs (see pages 93 and 95) had been introduced. To separate ore efficiently, hotching tubs had to be filled with graded material with pieces all about the same size. Grating the bouse from the mine before hotching served two functions: it washed off surface dirt and muck, and it began the sizing process. The cast iron bars of the grating were spaced about half an inch apart. Bouse was raked across the grating in a stream of water and anything smaller than half an inch across fell through the bars to be carried by the flowing water into a box, not shown in this illustration. At intervals this gravel-sized material was dug from the box and barrowed to the hotching tubs. Anything which stayed on top of the grating, unless it was pure ore, had to be broken down further. It was put into kibbles and carried to the knockstone (see page 83). A kibble sits to the right of the washerman raking the bouse with his colrake. A second washerman barrows more bouse onto the grate. The latter is unusual in wearing trousers in the modern style rather than knee-breeches.

*Reference number 1985 – 2032 7. Pencil, ink and watercolour.*
*Inscribed in pencil in the top right 'hotching'.*
*Given the page number 7 in the partial index and called 'Grating'.*

Grating

# Untitled

It is not clear what this picture was going to depict. The seated workman seems to be holding a rod or bar, but for what purpose?

*Reference number 1985 – 2032  9. Pencil. Watermark 1805.*

# Brake

This is a hotching tub, also known as a brake sieve. It was introduced in the early years of the nineteenth century, was easy to construct of planks of wood and rapidly replaced the tub seen on page 85. The hotching tub could separate more ore in less time and with much less effort. Hotching tubs became universal on washing-floors. The principle is the same as the tub – a sieve full of broken bouse is agitated in a container of water. But here the broken bouse has first been roughly sized through the grate, and the sieve is much bigger than the sieve in the tub. It is suspended from the arms of a long pole known as a stang. The washerboy stands, raised on a bench, or in this case a large stone, at the other end of the stang, shaking it vigorously with short jerks whilst holding it above his head. This agitation 'fluidises' the bouse in the sieve and the heavier galena sinks to the bottom. After a few minutes the washerboy will lower the pole, raising the sieve out of the water. One of the two men standing by the hotching tub will scrape off the layers which have formed in the sieve, finding the all-important layer of galena at the bottom. Layers are skimmed off by a roughly half-mooned shape piece of wood called a limb or limp. This is probably what can be seen ready for action on the side of the tub and above the wheelbarrow. The finest material, falling through the sieve into the tub of water, will be dug out at intervals with the long-handled shovel and sent to the buddle for separation into ore and waste. It is not clear why there are two men at the hotching tub, but they seem to be enjoying a relaxed conversation while the boy works. Like other young men in the images he is following the modern fashion among working people for long trousers.

We can see that the artist has not been satisfied with the composition, changing the position of the washerboy holding the stang. There are also faint pencil lines behind the figure in the beige jacket, suggesting he was initially intended to stand much higher in the picture.

*Reference number 1985 – 2032 3. Pencil, ink and watercolour.*
*'Brake' and numbered 3, the page number given to this illustration in the partial index.*

Brake

# Untitled

A pencilled '6' in the top right-hand corner suggests this may have been considered for the numbered series but rejected. Another depiction of a hotching tub, this is a rather rudimentary illustration. The perspective is unsuccessful and the hotching tub itself is not drawn with any detail. We could construct a hotching tub from the one illustrated in the previous picture: horizontal planked sides, with vertical timbers set on the inside corners of the tub and the planks nailed to these corner posts. One could not understand such details from this drawing. Furthermore the artist has not been entirely successful in depicting the thickness of the arms of the stang. This artist is more interested in the people. These two are boys, not grown men, and are dressed in their old work clothes — the boy at the end of the stang with ragged trousers, the other lad with raggy bottoms to his breeches. Despite the absence of technical detail, the limp for skimming off the layers is clearly shown in this lad's right hand, as is the pile of material already skimmed from the sieve. Is this perhaps a picture, unsigned, by the unidentified 'J B'? Compare the style with J B's painting of two men filling ore sacks on page 131. Neither this illustration nor the hotching tub painting on the previous page has been given any context. In both pictures the artist has chosen to depict the single piece and its operators rather than a whole scene. In reality hotching tubs were part of a complex which included grates, knockstones, buddles and further hotching tubs.

*Reference number 1985 – 2032 62. Pen, ink and sepia wash, with blue wash. Watermark 1805. Smaller than most of the collection at 18.7 cm by 19.2 cm.*

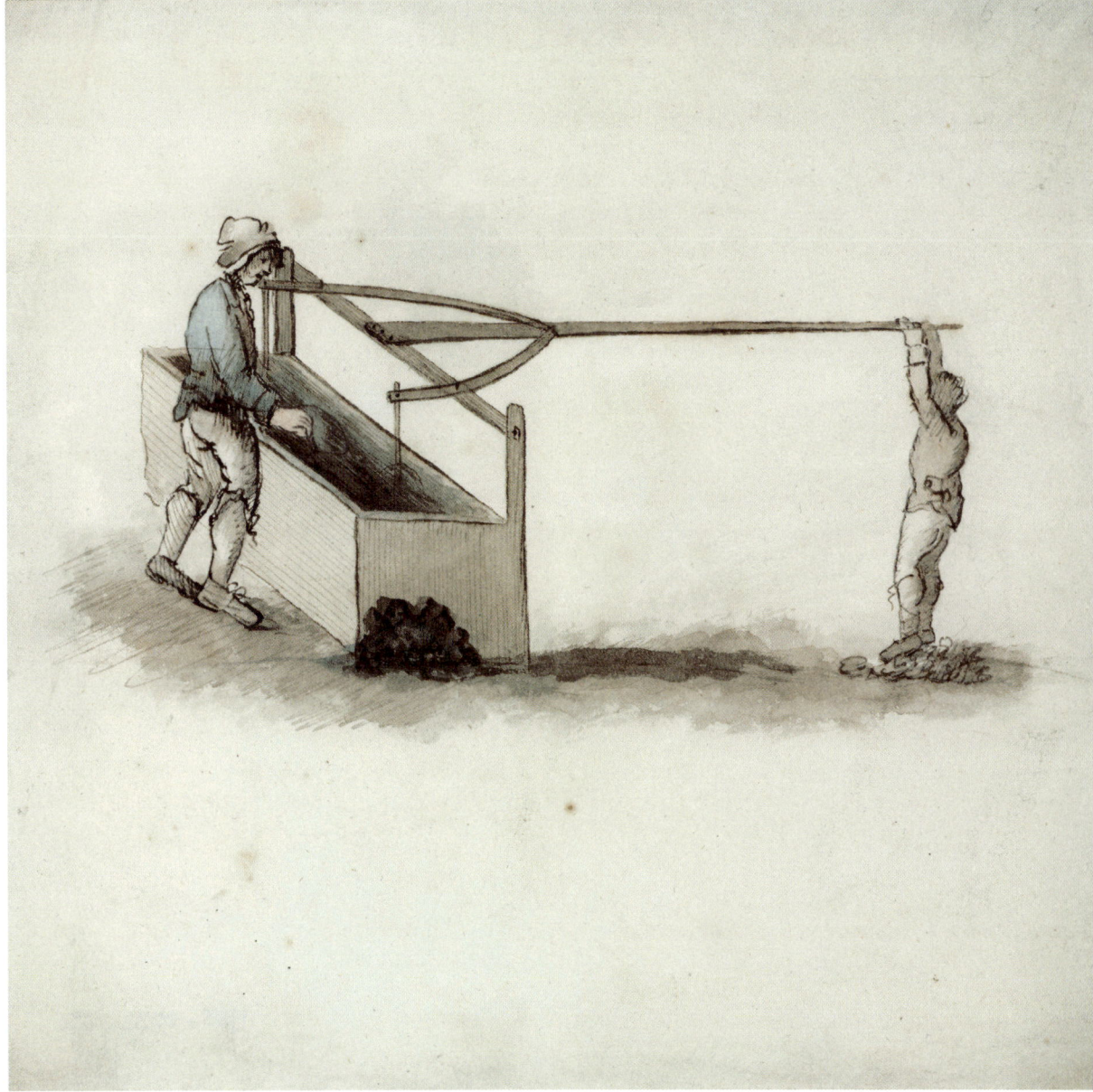

# Washers at Dinner, Wet Day

Here we have the context lacking in the two previous pictures. This, although largely unfinished, is the whole washing-floor. And we know when it was drawn. A date '1819' is all but hidden in the right foreground. Three men sheltering from the driving rain to eat their lunch are carefully observed and finished. Behind them, other figures and the scene of the washing-floor are sketched-in. The bouse teems in the background have a waggon on top. A hotching tub sits between the teems and the foreground, its handle, or stang, secured in the down position so the sieve can be emptied. A wheelbarrow sits in readiness and a kibble and shovel are lying about with an indication of heaps of bouse. Behind all, on the hillside, the whimsey at the mine can be made out in outline. The shelters for the men are called fleaks. The word fleak, for a portable shelter, is used in contemporary accounts, but this drawing is the only known illustration of what a fleak actually looked like. A simple wooden frame, its covering might be straw or heather or brushwood. It is difficult to be sure. Although we are unable to make out what they are eating, the composition of the three men sheltering under the fleak is beautifully realised. Flagons and bottles perhaps suggest alcoholic refreshment. For these men the respite from the rain is only temporary: soon they will be outside again in the open air, hotching and buddling.

*Reference number 1985 – 2032 40. Pencil, ink and sepia wash.*
*'Washers at Dinner' and underneath in a different ink and hand 'wet day'.*

Washers at Dinner

# Untitled

This finely-worked and finished study, and the next one, are both of a type, and perhaps suggest frontispieces or endpieces for the collection of drawings and paintings. Carefully composed, this picture shows tools characteristic of the washing-floor and for breaking stone. The wooden frame could be the bench for the knockstone or for the hotcher to stand on at the brake sieve. Arranged in front of it are the long-handled shovel and the colrake – universal tools of the washing-floor. Also included are the mell, or hammer, for breaking stone and, lying on the floor, a pair of wedges to be used with the mell (see page 119).

*Reference number 1985 – 2032 58. Ink and watercolour.*
*23.3 cm by 18.5 cm.*

# Untitled

Another elegant study of tools, this time those of mining and of the washing-floor. The finely drawn tub forms a centrepiece for the composition. Propped against it is the sieve or a shallow kibble. The tub is not as deep as the one on page 85, but this one too has a wooden spar across the top on which to rest the full sieve. The spade is unusual, for the pointed shovel illustrated elsewhere in this series is universally used above and below ground. The other tools are those of the miner. The pick is used wherever possible, as miners have to pay for any explosive they use. However whenever the rock is hard or has to be broken down, gunpowder is employed. Earlier pictures have demonstrated how two miners work together to drill holes for explosives with hammer and jumper or drill. This illustration shows a bundle of jumpers, similar to those strapped to the back of the climbing miner on page 67. After drilling the shot holes, miners charge them with gunpowder placed at the far end of the hole. The horn holds a supply of gunpowder. Once a suitable quantity of gunpowder has been placed in the hole it is filled up with clay or another inert material which is rammed in tight with a stemmer or tamper. The tool on top of the pick might be either the tool for charging the hole with gunpowder or the tamping tool. Before filling up the hole the miner inserts an iron or copper needle which reaches the gunpowder. Once the hole is tamped full, he withdraws the needle, leaving a hole down which he inserts his fuse until it reaches the powder. This tool is called a pricker and is lying across the bundle of jumpers. These prickers are iron: gradually they will be replaced with copper tools because an iron tool can strike a spark from rock, igniting the gunpowder prematurely. This is 'firing a shot in the hand' and is one of the commonest causes of accidents in the lead mines. The artist has chosen the tools for their composition as a group, reminiscent of a still life, rather than to show all the tools used either on the surface or underground.

*Reference number 1985 – 2032 54. Ink with grey and sepia wash. Watermark 1805.*
*Like the previous picture, slightly smaller than most at 23.3 cm by 18.5 cm.*

# Untitled

Unfinished, these are simple, small sketches of tools and equipment used by lead miners and lead ore washers. Are they little memory joggers, drawn from real life, to be included in pictures later on? Do they form raw material for the fine illustrations on the previous two pages? At the top of the left-hand column is a crossed shovel and colrake as used in buddling. Below this doodle are: a very elementary line drawing of a typical wheelbarrow, what looks like a simple sketch of the tub used in tubbing, two different types of kibble or bucket and then two further indeterminate little drawings, of which the bottom one may well give the proportions of a hotching tub and arm. The right-hand column is topped by a bucker for breaking ore, followed by a series of tools for use underground. First is a pick, then a scraper for cleaning debris out of shot holes. The next tool is uncertain and the following one looks like a jumper or hand drill. A different style of pick comes next, followed by the hammer used by pairs of men when hand-drilling. The final drawing may represent a powder horn for holding gunpowder, but this is by no means certain.

*Reference number 1985 – 2032 52. Pencil.*

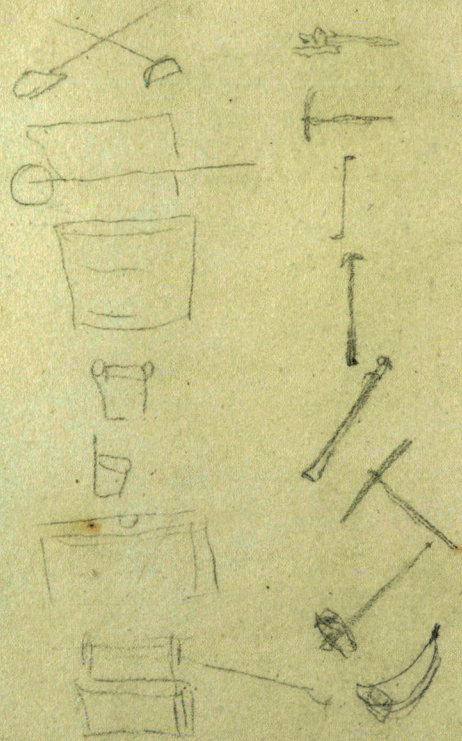

# Stamp Mill

This picture demonstrates the layout of a stamp mill. Stamp mills pounded material to the consistency of sand and were widely used in the tin-mining districts of Cornwall and Devon to pulverise ores. In the North Pennines, where the ore was less finely disseminated in the vein and where the lead smelters struggled to deal with finely ground ore, stamps were not used for crushing ore. Instead, from the eighteenth century onwards, stamps were often added to the equipment at smelt mills. Here, they crushed slags from the smelting hearths so they could be washed and resmelted to extract the lead which remained within them. Stamps were simple, noisy and effective. In the picture a waterwheel turns an axle with a series of cams on it. The cams lift heavy wooden posts shod with pieces of iron. These posts are held securely in a robust wooden frame. As the axle continues to revolve, the posts fall under their own weight, pounding and pulverising the material beneath them. Here, there are six stamps, three either side of the waterwheel. The different heights of the tops of the stamps show that they rise and fall in a rhythmical sequence rather than all at the same time. Once pulverised to the fineness required, the stamped material flows out through the grating shown in the stonework to the right. There is no indication whether this drawing and the next have been made at a specific smelt mill or are theoretical drawings demonstrating a typical layout. Both are in the small handful of pictures in the collection that show neither men nor horses. This picture is also one of the very few to be signed. 'T C' is inscribed in ink and very faintly in pencil. Are these the initials of Thomas Crawhall, the brother of William the Allenheads mine agent and Joseph the ropemaker and amateur artist? Thomas Crawhall worked in WB Lead's Newcastle office.

*Reference number 1985 – 2032 38. Pencil, ink, grey and yellow wash. Watermark 1805.*

T.C.

Stamp Mill

# Front view of a stamp mill

A waterwheel shown end-on, with three stamps on either side. The design and layout of the stamp mill is identical to that of the previous picture. The shadow of the waterwheel – the axle, three spokes and part of the rim – falls across the right-hand set of stamps. Has painting this arrangement been a technical exercise by the artist to show how he can depict a waterwheel? Like the vast majority of waterwheels in the lead mine district this one is shown as overshot. A water trough feeds a steady flow of water to the top of the wheel to fill the buckets.

*Reference number 1985 – 2032 64. Ink and wash.*
*Smaller than most pages at 20.3 cm by 17.3 cm.*

FRONT VIEW OF A STAMP MILL.

# Untitled, but given a number '32'

There is little to say about this sketch of a seated figure. Whatever the artist had in mind he never developed into a full picture. The reverse of this paper is even more frustrating — if only he had finished this one! James Mulcaster drew in plan and section, and described in great detail, the various types of smelting hearth in his paper written a few years before this series of pictures. Yet he did not show the interior or layout of a smelt mill, nor did he show smelters at work. After Mulcaster we do not find such an illustration until well into the era of photography. There is a solitary photograph of the inside of Rookhope mill, which was probably taken in the early years of the twentieth century. It is striking how little the scene at Rookhope has changed from this illustration of an unknown smelt mill drawn one hundred years earlier. Although this sketch is frustratingly very incomplete, the artist has done enough to let us see that this is a typical ore hearth for smelting lead, housed under a substantial stone arch. Behind the arch the fumes and smoke from the hearth are conducted into flues and away to a chimney. In front of the hearth itself is the workstone, the slightly inclined cast iron slab upon which the smelter turns and works the semi-molten mass of ore until hot, liquid lead trickles into the pot set below to catch it. In front of the pot are the moulds into which smelters pour hot lead to cool and solidify into pieces or pigs, each weighing eight or eleven stones (about 51 or 70 kilos). The tools for working the hearth, and the ladle for pouring the molten metal, are propped against the wall to the left of the hearth. A typical North Pennine smelt mill of the Regency period has a number of these hearths, as well as slag hearths for resmelting slags and perhaps a couple of the recently-introduced roasting hearths to give a preliminary roasting to the ores. Although no paintings of the interior of North Pennine smelting mills at this period exist, there is a slightly earlier and rather fine painting of a smelt mill interior in the Scottish National Portrait Gallery. This is one of four paintings of lead processing and smelting by David Allan, painted around 1780, and shows the mill at Leadhills in Lanarkshire. See page 14.[13]

*Reference number 1985 — 2032 29. Pencil. Verso: Pencil.*

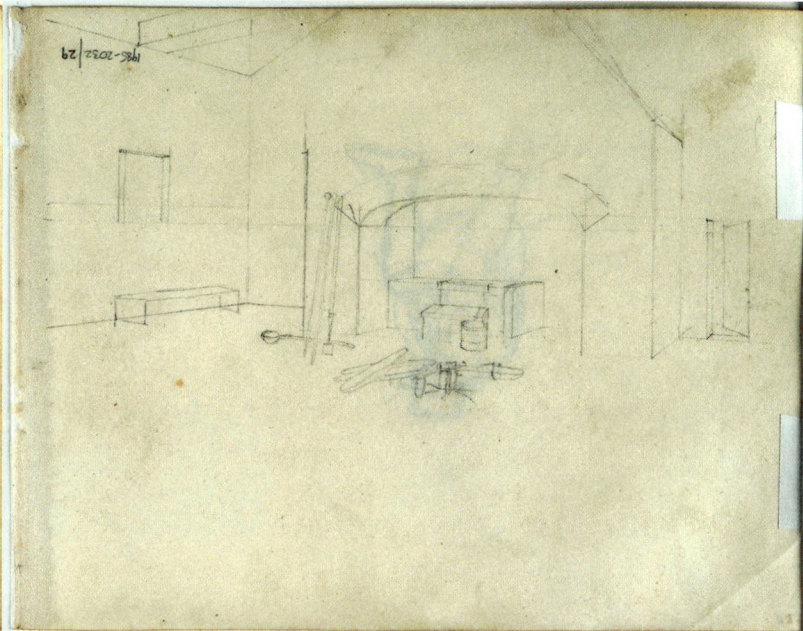

# Carrying Wood, Woodmen

We have moved away from drawings of processes and equipment and come back to people. Not now the miners and washermen and boys, but the others whose largely unacknowledged work kept production flowing. The lead mining industry required large numbers of men and boys working as labourers and in specialist trades to support the miners. These included blacksmiths to sharpen the tools, make minor repairs and keep the ponies shod. There were rail layers to lay the track in the mines. There were blowers, usually boys, turning ventilation fans underground. There were quarrymen, quarrying building stone. There were stone masons, lining the levels and shafts with stone and putting up buildings and structures as required. There were numerous joiners making wheelbarrows, ladders, hotching tubs, buddles and so on.

Most of these trades are not represented in our pictures. However this watercolour is one of a couple of exceptions. It shows two men carrying roughly-squared pieces of timber to the mine. As 'woodmen' these two are probably not skilled joiners, but their work is nevertheless crucial. They set roof supports and build stagings or platforms in the mine for the miners to work off. The man on the left carries one of the tools of his trade – an axe – in his belt. Perhaps the mine is the indistinct feature in the distance to the right of the first man. A very similar feature appears in the picture on page 87. Like many of the pictures, these are nicely judged character studies. One can feel the weight of the wood and the length of the journey these two have trudged.

*Reference number 1985 – 2032 19. Pencil, ink and watercolour. Watermark 1805.*
*Given the title 'Carrying Wood' and included in the partial index as page number 22.*

Carrying Wood

Woodmen

# Serving Masons

This picture illustrates another essential ancillary trade. Stonemasons lined the mine tunnels, or levels, built the structures on the washing-floors and constructed mineshops or lodging houses for miners to live in at distant mines during the week. Perhaps this is what they are building here, or perhaps it is simply a house. Stonemasons were skilled craftsmen, paid by the day and they were amongst the highest-paid workers in the lead industry. Like many in this collection of drawings and paintings, this is a quick sketch rather than a finished drawing. Perhaps the men carrying blocks of undressed stone on a stretcher have caught the artist's eye and he has dashed-off a rapid study. Some very light pencil lines show that the man at the rear was originally going to be depicted wearing a hat. In the background a mason is on the scaffolding dressing stone, another is laying stone and a third is about to ascend the ladder with more stone.

*Reference number 1985 — 2032 26. Ink, some pencil. Watermark 1805.*
*Given page number 29 and the title 'Carrying Stones' in the partial index.*

Serving Masons

# Dinner

This pleasing little ink and watercolour wash sketch shows a worker stopping to eat his midday meal with a cloth across his lap and a knife in his hand. Perhaps his dinner was tied up in a bundle which he has unwrapped, spreading the cloth out. He is wearing long trousers rather than the more common knee-breeches worn by most of the men in these pictures. At first glance he looks to be alone, but he is not.

Although only one figure is finished there are two more workmen sketched in outline behind him. One is sitting and drinking from a flagon and the other standing over him with arms outstretched for the bottle. Miners, of course, would have eaten underground, so these are surface workers.

*Reference number 1985 — 2032 46. Pencil, ink and sepia wash.*
*Page number 51 in the partial index.*

Dinner

# Gavelock

'Gavelock' is the dalesman's dialect name for a crowbar and this and the next two pictures illustrate quarrying rather than mining. The scene, yet another quick and unfinished sketch, like 'Serving Masons' on page 113 , speaks for itself. The supervisor, elegantly dressed with the pose of authority – and the hat to match – seems to wonder why the straining labourers are struggling so much to shift this giant lump of stone with their crowbars.

*Reference number 1985 – 2032 27. Pencil, pen and ink. Watermark 1805.*
*This picture is included in the partial index with page number 30.*

Gavelock

# Wedge

This is one of the watercolours that the artist has completed as a finished study and it makes a pleasing composition. A man swings his hammer, or mell, to split a large piece of rock with a wedge, whilst another watches intently, clay pipe in mouth. A few men smoke pipes in these pictures, but the habit is by no means universal. Are these large pieces of rock lying on a quarry floor? There is no background to give us any clues. The stone is painted as bedded in layers, so this is sandstone which will be used for building. The wedge has been carefully placed to split the rock along one of the bedding planes. The tools lying casually on the ground are very like the tools represented on page 101. These are the tools normally associated with leadminers: the powder horn for gunpowder, the pricker, the long spoon for charging drill holes with gunpowder and the pickaxe. However quarrymen will have used similar tools when they needed to blast and break rock with gunpowder, as shown in the next illustration.

*Reference number 1985 – 2032 27. Pencil, pen and ink. Watermark 1805.*
*This picture is included in the partial index with page number 30.*

Wedge

# Setting fire to match, Blasting

In this scene the rock looks like a cleaned quarry face, with the overburden of soil and subsoil removed from the top. However the foreground is unusually green and vegetated for a quarry floor, with no debris or broken rock lying about. Once again it is the person and the action which the artist wishes to capture rather than a fully-realised industrial landscape. The quarryman in the foreground has drilled and charged his shot hole and now it is time for blasting. He is concentrating hard on applying his light to the fuse which protrudes from the rock face, and which is already fizzing. He wears the soft hat which we have seen most of the miners wearing. There is drama and humour in the scene as a second figure waits crouching round the corner, peering out expectantly and waiting for the explosion.

*Reference number 1985 – 2032 37. Pencil, ink and watercolour.*
*Number 41 in the partial index where it is listed as 'Blasting, setting fire to match'.*

Setting fire to match
Blasting

# Crack, Partnership

Particularly striking in paintings such as this one is not just the individual character caught in every single different face, but the colourful clothes these ordinary miners of Regency England wear. This is not the drab brown or grey costume we associate with the working man of Victorian England, but an altogether more vibrant collection of jackets, waistcoats and neckties. Although the group has been subtitled 'Partnership' in pencil, and therefore represents a gang of miners who work together, the odd number – seven – is unusual. Partnerships were usually made up of even numbers, as the men generally worked underground in pairs. Partnerships were often family groups or close friends, and strong bonds were formed by working together underground. Something of their camaraderie is apparent in this snapshot of men relaxing, hands in pockets and gossiping. 'Crack' is dialect for conversation and this group is clearly enjoying 'a bit crack'. As noted previously, smoking is not common in these depictions of working life in the early nineteenth century; only one of the men has a pipe, with a splendid billow of smoke rising above his head. The composition is accomplished. Two men at either end stand in profile, directing the viewer into the group. Each man is well spaced in relation to the others. Every coat, every pair of breeches, every waistcoat is a different colour. The picture is full of human interest. Given the range of faces and expressions it is hard to resist the conclusion that these are real miners, drawn from life.

*Reference number 1985 2032 48. Pencil, ink and watercolour.*
*Inscribed 'Partnership' in pencil beneath the inked title of 'Crack'.*
*Numbered in top right corner 55, and the illustration's title 'Crack' has been added in pencil*
*at the bottom of the partial index.*

## 55

Crack
Partnership

# Wrestling, Sports

Sports were important to lead miners, both as spectacle and as games to take part in. Cumberland and Westmorland wrestling, as shown here, was followed avidly. A letter from Weardale, written in 1853, talks of everyone going to Newcastle, more than thirty miles away, to watch the wrestling.[14] Wrestling was also of course an opportunity for gambling. Here, two men (are they miners or professional wrestlers?) are locked together in a hold while all around them a group of spectators is unfinished but forms a ghostly presence at least twenty strong. If completed, this would have been a packed picture. Perhaps the artist realised he would not be able to get the balance right between foreground wrestlers and background audience and abandoned the painting. The spectators form a semi-circle standing and kneeling round the combatants and we can guess that much money rests on the outcome of this bout. Lead miners are usually portrayed by historians as a sober and serious class of men, devoutly Christian and expressing this religious belief through attendance at Methodist chapels. Whilst this is largely true for the miners of the high Victorian age, the early nineteenth century was a very different era with different social and moral values. The North Pennines lead miners of the Regency period were rough, tough and often hard-drinking men.

*Reference number 1985 – 2032 17. Pencil, ink and watercolour. Watermark 1805.*

Wrestling
Sports

# Effects of Alston Brewery

This picture has been given several different titles. 'Effects of Alston Brewery' is the main title, but 'of Alston Brewery' has been scored through and the more neutral 'Drinking' substituted. The original faint pencil title is 'Battle', and 'Pay Day' has also been added in a different hand. Put them all together and the titles tell a story. Lead miners were paid only once a year at this time. However they received a regular monthly sum called lent money as a minimum subsistence wage. At the end of the year there was a grand reckoning-up of the value of the lead ore each partnership had raised and of the expenses in candles, explosives and so on that they had incurred. Finally, the year's lent money was deducted from the balance and if a miner had earned more than enough to cover both his costs and his lent money he was handed this cash at the Pays. At the Pays, too, were the tradesmen who had extended credit to mining families for groceries, clothes and other goods and they in turn were paid as the miners settled their bills. Individual pays varied wildly. The fortunate miner found himself with a large pile of notes and coins, whilst the unfortunate ended the year in debt. Pay day was a big day in the annual calendar and much drinking took place. Here we have a vivid illustration of a pay day ending all too predictably in a drunken brawl between two miners. The place is clearly real, a cobbled square outside J Dawson's hotel and public house, and is almost certainly Allenheads. See page 6 for more about Dawson and Allenheads. A nice little detail is the mounting block outside the hotel to the right of the door. The hotel, like most of the bigger buildings at the time, is roofed with stone slates. The little single-storey building behind it has the traditional roof covering of poorer houses – heather thatch. The alteration in the picture's title suggests some squeamishness about using the name 'Alston Brewery'. Alston Brewery was a business in which a number of the agents of W B Lead and other mine businesses had shares and maybe the artist drew back from causing offence to some of the more important people in local society.

*Reference number 1985 – 2032 49. Pencil, ink, touches of red ink. Watermark 1805.*

## 56

Drinking

Effects of Alston Brewery          Pay day

# Filling and Weighing Ore, Carriers

The next group of images contains some of the most important illustrations in the collection. We can find elsewhere descriptions and a few illustrations of early-nineteenth century ore separation, but until these pictures came to light there was not a single known image showing the carriage of lead ore by pack pony. Nor had we seen details such as ore sacks, harness and saddles. These pictures thus shed great light on a neglected but important element of the lead mining industry. Lead mines were often in remote high places where roads were bad or non-existent. There are many contemporary complaints about the state of the roads and the sheer difficulty of travelling around the North Pennines. Poor roads and rough tracks meant that horses and carts were often not a realistic option for carrying lead ore from the mines to the lead smelting mills. Instead, the ore had to be transported – and in huge quantities every year – on the backs of pack ponies. As each pony carried only two hundredweight (one tenth of a ton) this was an enormous endeavour. This picture shows the beginning of the journey at the washing-floor. A large heap of washed, or dressed, lead ore, cleaned and ready for smelting, lies against the stone wall across the left-hand half of the picture. A group of ponies waits on the right to be laden, whilst the carrier's dog sensibly takes the opportunity for a nap. Two of the men – it is uncertain whether it is the carriers or other workers who have this task – are busy filling the sacks which the ponies will carry. In the centre, the weigh beam is set up to check each bag contains the correct weight of ore. A weight sits on the left-hand platform and the sacks will be lifted one by one onto the right-hand platform of the scales. One can perhaps assume that it is the job of the man on the right to carry the filled sacks to the scales, weigh them off and tie the tops. He has a kibble beside him, from which he can add more ore to bring the bag to the correct weight or he will take some ore out if the bag is too heavy. The very large number of filled bags suggests the scale of the transport required.

*Reference number 1985 – 2032 5. Pencil, ink and watercolour.*
*Given the number 5, which is the page number allocated to this picture in the partial index*
*where it is called 'Weighing and Filling Ore'.*

Filling & Weighing Ore
Carriers

# Untitled

This study shows a scene similar to that of the previous picture, but here the artist is concentrating on the two men filling the sacks. It is in a different style, with much use of hatching, and although not signed was probably drawn and painted by 'J B'. See the next page. The scene is set on a plateau, with no other evidence of mining or ore washing around. In reality the men will have been surrounded by the busy scene of a washing-floor but the artist, wanting to focus on the single action of filling sacks, has painted a simple generic background. The weigh beam is again prominent. This is the only time in the whole process of mining and washing when the amount of ore produced is weighed, so the weigh beam, or baulk, is an important feature. Filling each sack to the correct weight allows the agents to record accurately the amount of lead ore sent away for smelting. Not only does this determine how much the miners are paid (for they are paid only for pure ore) but the lead smelting agents will keep a record of how many bags of ore are needed to make a 'fodder' (21 hundredweight or 1,066 kilos) of smelted lead. In this way they keep a check on the efficiency of each smelt mill.

*Reference number 1985 — 2032 60. Pen, ink and watercolour.*
*A smaller picture at 19.7 cm by 18.5 cm.*

# Untitled

This sketch must be a preliminary study for the previous picture. The initials J B are in ink and seem to have been added later. They presumably refer to the artist. They may be over an earlier, now indistinct, signature. To date the owner of the initials has not been identified so 'JB' remains unknown, although he might have been one of the group of friends who made up the Gorcock Club. See page 24. The drawing gives us an insight into this artist's way of working. He gets the figures right and then adds the background. This suggests that the scene was not completed from life on the spot but in the studio. See also the illustration of a boy with a barrow on page 75.

*Reference number 1985 — 2032 34 Pencil. Watermark 1805.*
*The signature 'JB' in ink.*

# Carrying Galloways

This is an important picture for it shows not just a group of pack ponies but also the wooden saddles they wear to carry the sacks of lead ore. 'Galloway' is the name given to small sturdy horses such as these. Every pony will carry two of the long sacks shown in previous pictures, and each sack weighs one hundredweight, or one twentieth of a ton. The artist, accomplished at drawing animals, has captured not just the character of the individual beasts but a sense of the poor quality of some of the ponies used by the ore carriers. The animal with its rear quarters facing us is particularly bony and undernourished. Ore carriers were not employed by W B Lead (the Beaumonts) or any of the other lead mining and smelting businesses, but were self-employed contractors. Their work was seasonal, as the carrier routes became impassable quagmires in the winter months. Carriage generally started in April and closed down in September or October. This extremely short season put immense pressure on the carriers to get the ore down to the smelt mills by all possible means to build up stocks for winter smelting. The prominent brand 'J C' on the flank of the foremost pony is tantalising. No other horse in any of the pictures is shown as branded. It is hard to resist the conclusion that the initials are those of the artist, Joseph Crawhall.

*Reference number 1985 – 2032 23. Pencil, pen and ink, with sepia wash.*
*This is probably the picture titled 'Galloways' and given page number 26 in the partial index.*

Carrying Galloways

# Loading Galloways

This wonderful illustration tells us a great deal about lead carriage. This and the next two pictures are finished illustrations and can be read as a series. Here, the sacks have been filled and the carrier, red-faced with the effort, is beginning to load his string of Galloway ponies. The unit of weight used in the lead industry was a 'bing' of eight hundredweight (about 406 kilos) and the subdivision of a bing was a 'horse' of two hundredweight (just over 101 kilos). A 'horse' was the weight carried by one pony. Thus in two sacks of lead ore each pony carried 16 stone, the equivalent of a heavy person. Stop for a moment to consider the thousands of tons of lead ore mined and smelted each year. Ten ponies (about the number shown in this picture) were required to transport a single ton of lead ore from a mine to the smelt mill. The sheer volume of traffic trudging across the hills every summer was immense and the logistical problems enormous. The wooden saddle is drawn very precisely in this picture, and the blanket it rests on can also be seen. These are sturdy little ponies, the forerunners of the Dales and Fell breeds. Sometimes the ponies were muzzled before they set off on their journey and in this picture the muzzle can be seen below the noses of all of them. It is sometimes said that the muzzles were to prevent ponies eating grass poisoned by lead ore leaking from the sacks. It seems more likely that they were to prevent any ponies stopping to nibble grass along the route and slowing down the whole pack train.

*Reference number 1985 – 2032 36. Ink and watercolour.*
*The number 40 refers to the page number in the partial index where this picture is called*
*'Carrier Galloways, loading'.*

*Loading Galloways.*

# Driving Galloways

This is the only known illustration of a pack train in the North Pennines. It shows that the ponies were not tied together in a string, but ambled along as a group with their reins loose on their backs. In this case they are not shown with muzzles. There is no need to tie the sacks to the wooden saddles for their weight keeps them in place. The picture does not show a full train, which probably consisted of ten or a dozen or more animals. Behind the animals the drover and his dog keep the train moving on. The animal being nipped by the dog is a donkey and in front of the donkey the next pony is a bag of bones, demonstrating that any serviceable animal was pressed into use to get the ore to the mills. The carrier ways over the fells were not paved and the horses had to pick their way across ground which must have turned to a deep morass of bog towards the end of the carriage season. Carrier routes can still be walked over the North Pennine fells as most are now public rights of way or cross open access land. They do not follow the valleys but instead march straight across the high hills, taking the shortest route between mine and mill.

*Reference number 1985 — 2032 24. Pencil, pen, ink and watercolour. Watermark 1805.*
*Number 27 is the page number against this picture in the partial index where it is called*
*'Carrier Galloways, Driving'.*

*Driving Galloways*

# Galloways carrying Wood

Here, the pack train is travelling from right to left, rather than as in the previous picture from left to right. This can be interpreted as the reverse journey back from the smelt mill to the mine. The return journey was not wasted as it was used for 'back carriage' of materials needed at the mine. The ponies are loaded with bundles of wood, perhaps destined to form roof supports underground. They are carrying one bundle on each side and one slung across their back. Only one pony is sporting a muzzle, but is not wearing it over the nose. As in the previous picture, the carrier and his dog bring up the rear, keeping the animals moving.

The carrier's pose suggests a nonchalant cockiness. He knows that the industry cannot do without him and that the various lead businesses are likely to compete to retain him and his animals. Several carriers were tenants of, and thereby tied to, the Beaumont family, holding small farms in Allendale and Weardale and on the Winlaton estate near Tyneside. Many more had no direct obligations to WB or other lead businesses. They could pick and choose who they worked for. Their landlords often demanded high rents for small farms where horses were kept because they knew that lead carriers could make a very good living.

*Reference number 1985 — 2032 41. Pencil, ink and watercolour.*
*In the partial index it is identified as 'Galloways, carrying wood' and given page number 45.*

Galloways carrying Wood.

# Ore Cart

This is another unique illustration. A fine study in subdued browns it shows not an ore cart but a lead cart. It is the only known illustration of a lead cart – a sight which would have been extremely common on the lead routes between the smelt mills and the wharves on the River Tyne at Blaydon, upriver from Newcastle. Clearly visible on the back of the cart is a piece, or pig, of lead. The lead is inscribed 'W Blackett' which was the name used on lead made by both the Blacketts and their successors, the Beaumonts. The letters 'W.Blackett' were raised in reverse on the inside of the cast iron moulds into which hot, liquid lead was poured after smelting, thus appearing on the cooled and solidified lead piece as incised lettering. Some pieces of lead with this exact lettering have survived to the present day. Each of these carts carried ten such pieces, of either eight or eleven stone each (about 51 or 70 kilos). Thus a cart carried half a ton of lead or slightly more. The surviving letter books of the Blackett and Beaumont business from the eighteenth and early nineteenth centuries are full of letters about the carriers and the problems they caused. Often they picked up a load of lead from the smelt mill, carried it a short distance and offloaded it by the roadside before going back for another load. Piles of lead could be stuck in transit for months. This caused real difficulty at times of rising lead prices when the mining businesses needed their lead urgently down at the Tyne, for sale and onward shipment. When all the mining businesses wanted their lead carried at the same time the carriers were in an immensely strong bargaining position. It was not until the coming of the railways in the 1830s that the power and monopoly of the carriers was finally and fatally undermined. The initials 'J C' are partially hidden on the horse's blinker – is this the signature of the artist Joseph Crawhall? Also scrawled on the picture is 'this revers'd' in pencil. Does this instruction suggest an intention to copy the picture as a mirror image for etching and then printing the correct way round?

*Reference number 1985 – 2032 39. Pencil, ink and sepia wash. Watermark 1805.*
*Titled 'Ore Cart' in pencil rather than in ink.*

The Cart.

# Untitled

This illustration provides the only known visual reference to lead being carried by pack ponies rather than on a cart. Laden with two pieces of lead, one strapped on either side of the saddle, these ponies are bearing the same weight as those carrying sacks of lead ore – 16 stone, or a tenth of a ton. Some of the carrier ways leading from the more remote smelt mills high in the hills became impassable for carts for much of the year. At these times pack ponies were the only possible means of moving lead. Hundreds of ponies must have been kept on the small farms in and around the North Pennines. An inventory of John Chatt's farm, at Peacock House in Hexhamshire, gives us an insight into these smallholdings. John Chatt kept and bred Galloway ponies. When he died in 1789 his farm stock consisted mostly of horses. He had only four cows and a calf valued at £16, but more significantly three mares, eight Galloways and three foals, together valued at £52.[15]

*Reference Number 1985 – 2032 61. Pen and line, some pencil.*
*19 cm by 20 cm.*

# From Life

An unfinished pencil sketch of a pony, evidently drawn from life. This drawing is on the reverse side of another very incomplete drawing called 'On the Tyne'. The men and women who kept and worked these carrier ponies had a formidable reputation for brute strength. *"There was John Jackson, who lived at Sparty Lea and kept sometimes eight and sometimes ten ponies, and a mule which he called 'his devil', as it was very wicked and bad to lead; but Jackson being a low, thick, and exceedingly strong man,* *used to hold the mule by main force while he threw the two bags of ore on to its back. When the weather was fair, Betty, his wife, had to go with him to catch the ponies, while he was loading them. I have often seen her riding on the back of these ponies, with a man's weather-beaten hat on her head. Jackson was not satisfied with his day's work with the galloways, but went to pump water in the mines at night; and it has always been a saying that nobody beat the world with hard work in Allendale but Jackson…".*[16]

*Reference number 1985 – 2032 50 verso. Watermark 1805.*

from life

1985-2032/50

# November 5th 1813

This is the only one of the collection of pictures which we are certain depicts an actual event. Thomas Wentworth Beaumont turned 21 in 1813 and his coming of age was celebrated with great gusto across the mining districts of Weardale and Allendale. His parents, Colonel Thomas and Mrs Diana Beaumont, supplied all their miners with copious quantities of free beer and numerous pot mugs inscribed with the date were also produced and distributed. The result of this liberality was an occasion which went down in legend as 'the Great Drink'.[17] The spirit of the day is captured in this humorous rendering. Drinking from their November 5th mugs, vomiting, urinating, fighting, dancing or simply collapsing, the miners are making the most of their employers' generosity. Nowadays we tend to view lead miners through the lens of late-Victorian propriety. When Arthur Raistrick, a twentieth-century historian of lead mining, was shown this picture he refused to accept that it showed lead miners. In his opinion lead miners did not behave like this. Later in the nineteenth century, in high Victorian times, after Methodism had become the dominant form of Christianity, this was true. The next majority of a son of the Beaumonts, that of Wentworth Blackett Beaumont in 1850, was celebrated with tea served by young ladies dressed in white. But this picture takes us back to an older, rougher, wilder society.

*Reference number 1985 – 2032 18. Pencil, pen and line, with sepia wash. Watermark 1805*

November 5.th 1813

# Untitled

The purpose of this carefully made illustration is now lost. All that can be said is that it depicts a set of double-acting bellows of unusual design. Perhaps it is a fantasy, or invention of the artist?

*Reference number 1985 — 2032 55. Ink and wash.*
*22.5 cm by 18.7 cm, so slightly smaller than most of the pictures.*

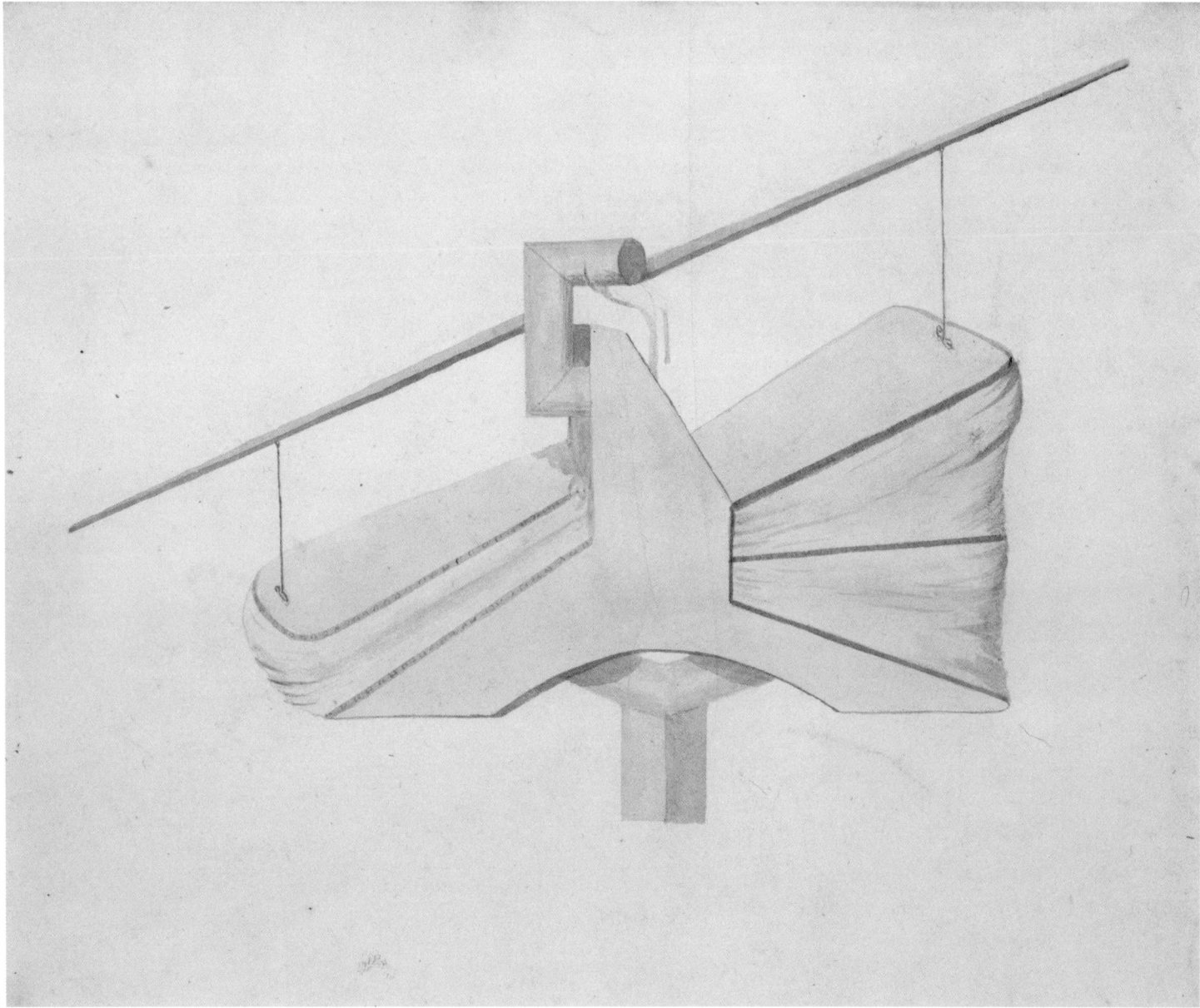

# Pitmen

The cross-section of a nineteenth-century coal seam serves to reinforce the value of the other pictures in the series. This view of a group of coal hewers is familiar to us from illustrations elsewhere. The lead mining pictures are not familiar, for the life of lead miners during the Regency period is not captured apart from through the pictures in this book. It is not understood why this unfinished image is included in the collection. There are coal seams in the upper geological strata of the North Pennines and coal was mined in the lead mining district, particularly on Alston Moor. Yet the coal seams of the Pennines are thin, not like the seam shown here. The title is in a different hand to nearly all the others in the series, but may be in the same hand as 'Takeing a Bargain' on page 69.

*Reference number 1985 — 2032 30. Pen and ink with pencil.*

Seam

Pitmen

# Untitled

This picture, too, is something of a puzzle. A man pulls a tub along a rail track. There are no candles or other lights. Is he on the surface? The hat and jacket suggests he is, as do the shadows on the tub. What is in the tub? It does not look like a lead tub. Is it a coal tub? Why is 'no 4' in the top right-hand corner? This is dissimilar to the numbering on all the other pictures. This image reinforces the impression that the collection of drawings and watercolours bought by the Science Museum Library is not a coherent collection, but either work in progress or abandoned (so many of the pictures are unfinished) or the surviving remnant of a larger portfolio. Whichever it is does not detract from the importance of the collection to our understanding of North Pennine lead mining. Is this another illustration by 'J B'? The figure bears some similarity to those on pages 95 and 131.

*Reference number 1985 – 2032 65. Pencil, ink and wash.*
*19 cm by 19.5 cm.*

# On the Tyne

This pencil sketch is so unfinished that it is probably now impossible to identify whereabouts on the River Tyne it represents. It has been suggested that 'NB' on the shoreline on the left-hand side could mean 'North Bank' or 'Newburn Bank'. If the view shows the start of the northwards sweep of the Tyne looking east from Blaydon Green, the buildings sketched roughly on the right would be in the right place to be the W B Lead staiths and silver refinery site. However this is speculation. Better then to take this as a symbolic end to the sequence of pictures we have been following. Numbered 57, it is the highest numbered picture in the sequence, so perhaps was always intended to be the end of the journey. It tells us that the galena, or lead ore, mined from under the Pennine hills, separated out from other minerals on the washing-floor beside the mine, carried to the smelt mills and smelted into lead and then carried as pieces of lead down to the wharves on the river Tyne, has reached the end of its journey. From here, lead will be sold on as a raw material for industry or turned into sheets or pipes. Lead from the Pennines spawned a major lead manufacturing industry on Tyneside but it was also exported down the river to London and overseas to Holland, France and Germany and even into Russia. Both major North Pennine lead businesses, W B Lead and the London Lead Company, had wharves upriver from Newcastle, at Blaydon and Stella respectively. Lead poured down the lead roads to these points to be piled high on the quays by the thousands of pieces. Here, too, W B Lead had a silver refinery to extract silver as a valuable by-product from much of their lead. Silver refining was an important part of the business of both major lead concerns, the refining process producing not just silver but lead oxide, or litharge, which was also highly saleable. There is no reference to silver refining in these pictures.

*Reference number 1985 – 2032 50. Pencil. Watermark 1805.*

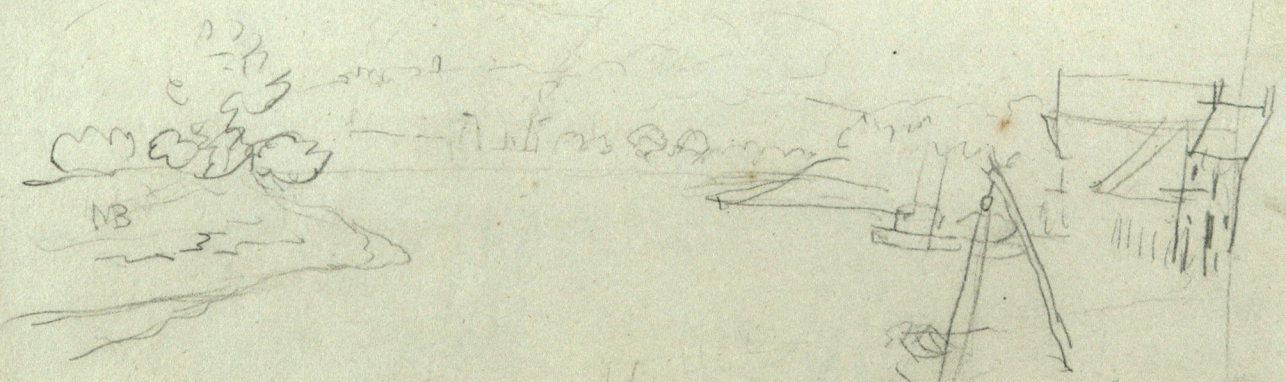

on the Tyne

# Untitled

This page shows two, untitled, sections of the same piece of apparatus. It is something of an anomaly in this collection of pictures. It is not a representation of a mining scene, but a technical drawing of an ore separation machine, accompanied by four pages of text describing the principle of ore separation and how the machine would work. As far as is known such a machine was never built. Certainly it never went into mass production. The author of the drawing has understood the process required to carry out ore separation and has had the ability to devise a piece of equipment and to draw it. Yet it is doubtful whether such a machine would have worked economically at a practical scale. The work is unsigned, so we cannot now know whose idea it was. It remains a curiosity.

*Reference number 1985 – 2032 67. Ink and wash.*

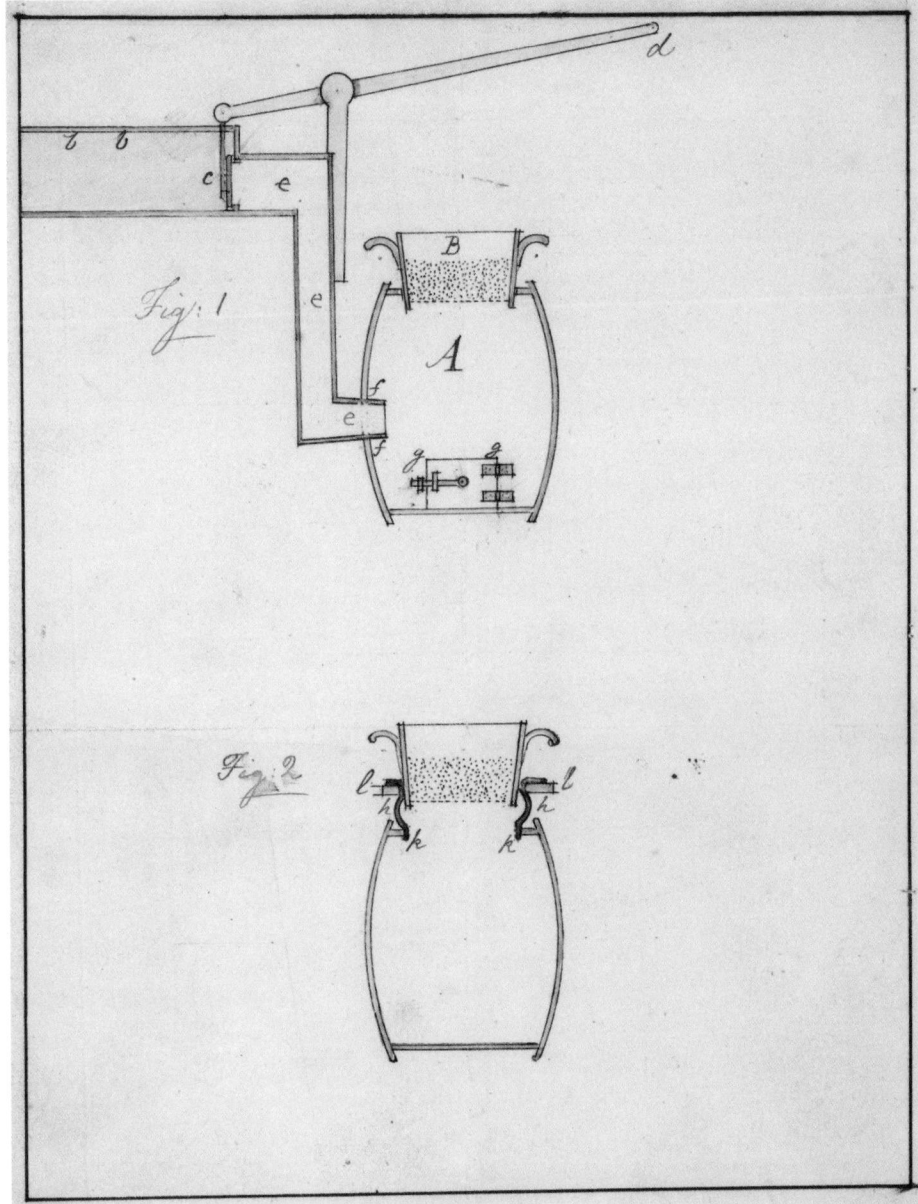

Fig: 1

Fig: 2

# On the Washing of Lead Ore

The text on the following four pages refers to the illustration on the previous page and has been transcribed in full.

*As it is only in consequence of its greater Specific Gravity that that Lead-Ore can be seperated (by any kind of washing) from the lighter matter with which it is mixed, many contrivances have been used to effect the necessary seperation; sometimes by plunging a Sieve containing such a mixture into Water with a Force which experience has taught the workmen is best suited for the purpose. Sometimes currents of Water are used, with a degree of force adapted to the fineness of the Mixture, since in a courser state a Current may be used which if applied to the mixture in a finer state wou'd carry away the whole, or great part of the Lead-Ore along with the mixture. But in this mode of washing also it is plane that the lighter particles of the matter washed will first be moved by the Stream, and the heavier only remain behind, so that neither of those modes cou'd succeed unless the Lead-Ore was heavier or had a greater Specific Gravity than the matter to be seperated by any Mode of Washing that can be used. — But to determine the fact and to ascertain how much the Lead-Ore exceeds the Weight of the Mixture generally to be seperated, I collected and determined by an accurate tryal of the specimins, I picked out of a mixture (in the hands of the Washers) the following specimins, and found the Specific Gravity to be as follows Viz.*

*----------------------------- Lead-Ore ---- 7.400 ------------------------*

*--------------------------- Calk ----------- 4.710------------------------*

*------------------------- Fluor Spar -------- 3.158 ----------------------*

*------------------------- LimeStone ---------2.600 ----------------------*

*Then on this principle I will suppose that a Vissil of any regular Figure be provided say a Cylindrical one of 5 or 6 Fut in Length filled with Water, and suppose a Sieve or other Cylindrical Vissil of 5 or 6 Inches in length be also provided of such a size as to easily sliped a little way within the first Cylinder, but so to fit as to allow no escape of any Water.   And suppose the bottom of this Lesser Vissil*

*Reference number 1985 — 2032 66*

# On the Washing of Lead-Ore

As it is only in consequence of its greater Specific Gravity that
that Lead-Ore can be seperated (by any kind of washing) from the
lighter matter with which it is mixed, many contrivances have been
used to effect the necessary seperation; sometimes by plunging a Sive
containing such a mixture into Water with a force which experience
has taught the the workmen is best suited for the purpose. Sometimes
currents of Water are used, with a degree of force adapted to the
fineness of the Mixture, since in a coarser state a Current may be
used which if applied to the mixture in a finer state would carry
away the whole, or great part of the Lead-Ore along with the mixture.
But in this mode of washing also it is plane that the lighter particles
of the matter washed will first be moved by the Stream, and the heavier
only remain behind, so that neither of those modes could succeed
unless the Lead-Ore was heavier or had a greater Specific Gravity
than the matter to be seperated by any Mode of Washing that can
be used. —— But to determine the fact and to ascertain how much
the Lead-Ore exceeds the Weight of the Mixture generally to be sepera=
ted, I collected and determined by an accurate tryal the specimens.
I picked out of a mixture (in the hands of the Washers) the following
specimens, and found the Specific Gravity to be as follows Vig.t

|                | |
|----------------|-------|
| Lead-Ore       | 7.400 |
| Calk           | 4.710 |
| Fluer Spar     | 3.158 |
| Lime Stone     | 2.600 |

Then on this princeple I will suppose that a Vessel of any regular
Figure be provided say a Cylindrical one of 5 or 6 Feet in Length
filled with Water, and suppose a Sive or other Cylindrical Vessel
of 5 or 6 Inches in length be also provided of such a size as to easily
sleped a little way within the first Cylinder, but so to fit as to allow
no escape of any Water. And suppose the bottom of this lesser Vessel,

Be covered with the mixture (from which the Lead-Ore is to be seperated) say to the thickness of 3 or 4 Inches, and when inserted into the top of the first mentioned Cylinder that the bottom which supports the mixture, be instantly removed; the contents of course will immediately begin to descend thro' the Water with different degrees of Velocity proportioned to the specific gravity, of the seperate particles, the heaviest moving the quickest & of course will first arrive at the bottom, where the mixture will be found in layers or strata taking place according to the gravity of the particles of which the mixture was composed. But as such a Vissil wou'd require to be emptied after every operation, tho' correct in its principle, wou'd be too tedious for practice. ----It remains then to be considered by what means this effect may be more easily imitated & perhaps improved, and instead of the mixture being allowed to descend thro the Water, the Water be made to pass thro' the mixture not only with an equal Velocity, but also with the power of increasing or diminishing it at pleasure as well as to remove the Lead-Ore, after the operation with less trouble, it is to be presumed, a more convenient Machine will be obtained. And such a machine may be constructed as follows.-----

Let A Fig: 1 be a common Barrel capable of holding Water, with a circular hole cut in the top, so as to admit the Conical Sieve

B. so closely fitted as to allow no water to escape by the side or in any manner but thro' the sieve containing the mixture to be washed the bottom of which is to be constructed of very fine Wire Work that will allow the Water to rise thro' it and thro' the mixture represented by the dotted marks. -

bb is the surface of the water to be employ'd, which by opening the shuttle C, by means of the Lever d will allow the Water to pass thro' the Wooden conduter, eee. into the Barrel A, thro' the round apperture ff, into which the conical end of the conducter

Reference number 1985 — 2032 66

Be covered with the mixture (from which the Lead-Ore is to be sepe=rated) say to the thickness of 3 or 4 Inches, and when inserted into the top of the first mentioned Cylinder that the bottom which supports the mixture, be instantly removed; the contents ofcourse will immediately begin to descend thro' the Water with different degrees of Velocity, proportioned to the specific gravity, of the separate particles, the heaviest moving the quickest & of course will first arrive at the bottom, where the mixture will be found in layers or strata taking place according to the Gravity of the particles of which the mixture was composed. But as such a Vessel would require to be emptied after every operation, tho' correct in its principle, would be too tedious for practice. — It remains then to be considered by what means this effect may be more easily imitated & perhaps im=proved, and instead of the mixture being allowed to descend thro' the Water, the Water be made to pass thro' the mixture not only with an equal Velocity, but also with the power of encreasing or diminishing it at pleasure as well as to remove the Lead Ore, after the operation with less trouble, it is to be presumed, a more convenient Machine will be obtained. And such a machine may be constructed as follows. —

Let A Fig: 1 be a common Barrel capable of holding Water, with a circular hole cut in the top, so as to admit the Conical Sieve

B so closely fitted as to allow no water to escape by the side or in any manner, but thro' the sieve containing the mixture to be washed the bottom of which is to be constructed of very fine Wire Work that will allow the Water to rise thro' it and thro' the mixture represented by the dotted marks.

bb is the surface of the water to be employ'd. which by opening the shuttle C, by means of the Lever d will allow the Water to pass thro' the Wooden conductor, eee. into the Barrel A, thro' the round apperture ff. into which the conical end of the conductor is to be so fitted as to allow no water to escape. Then the shuttle c being opened, the Water will immediately rush thro' the pipe eee into the Barrel A which when filled the water will press against the bottom of the mixture in the Sieve with a Force equal (or nearly equal to the perpendicular height of the head of Water at bb above the bottom of the Sieve, which will be very nearly equal to the Velocity which a heavy body wou'd require in falling thro' that space. And as this will be the greatest force which this Machine can yeild, this height must be proportioned to that force which experience will teach to be the greatest ever required. Any lesser force will be readily obtained, by, in part shutting off the Water, or occasionally closing the Shuttle whenever the Sieve B is removed. — Thus the Water will easily be made to move upwards and pass thro' the Mixture to be washed with any degree of force that may be required, as was proposed.---

g,g is a Door for the conveniency of cleaning out the sediment but must be so guarded with Leather &c. that when shutt and fixed in its place no Water can escape, This sediment will contain much Lead Ore, and must of Course be subjected to a a rewashing. — The sides of the Sieve may be cutt down to such a convenient debth, that the Water may flow over the edges, in such a manner as by practice may be found most convenient In addition to the Machine discribed, if a Leather Boot be added in the manner shown at Fig:2 it will allow the sieve to be raised or lowered a little at pleasure, or allow the Workman, to give the sieve a Circular motion, as is the practice at present when the sieve is used. — h h shows the section of the Leather Boot (tinged yellow) the lower edge at k k may be nailed to the edge of the Circular hole cutt in the head of the Cask. — l l is the section of a circular board with a Circular hole cutt thro' the middle, large

enough to admitt the Sieve with the thickness of the leather also, which may pass thro' the hole is turned back & nailed to the upper side of the

Reference number 1985 – 2032 66

164

is to be so fitted as to allow no water to escape. Then the shuttle c — being opened, the Water will immediately rush thro' the pipe ccc into the Barrel A which when filled the water will press against the bottom of the mixture in the Sieve with a force equal (or nearly equal to the perpendicular height of the head of Water at b b above the bottom of the Sieve, which will be very nearly equal to the Velocity which a heavy body wou'd acquire in falling thro' that space. And as this will be the greatest force which this Machine can yield, this height must be proportioned to that force which experience will teach to be the greatest ever required. Any lesser force will be readily obtained, by, in part shutting off the Water, or occasionally closing the Shuttle when ever the Sieve B is removed. —— Thus the Water will easily be made to move upwards and pass thro' the Mixture to be washed with any degree of force that may be required. as was proposed. —

g. g is a Door for the conveniency of cleaning out the sediment — but must be so guarded with Leather &c that when shutt and fixed in its place no Water can escape, This sediment will contain much Lead Ore. and must of Course be subjected to a rewashing. —— The sides of the Sieve may be cutt down to such a convenient debth. that the Water may flow over the edges, in such a manner as by practice may be found most convenient In addition to the Machine discribed, if a leather Boot be added in the manner shown at Fig: 2 it will allow the sieve to be raised or lowered a little at pleasure, or allow the Workman, to give the sieve a Circular motion. as is the practice at present when the sieve is used. — h h shows the section of the Leather Boot (tinged yellow) the lower edge at k k may be nailed to the edge of the Circular hole cutt in the head of the Cask. —— l l is the section of a circular board with a Circular hole cutt thro' the middle, large enough to admitt the Sieve with the thickness of the leather also, which may pass thro' the hole is turned back & nailed to the upper side of the

*Board in such a manner as to prevent the escape of any Water. — Any number of such Machines may be used one below the other as the fall will allow which at the places generally used for Washing the Ore will allow of almost any number of them if found convenient for the purposes designed. — And such Machines will be easily moved from one situation to another.---*

Board in such a manner as to prevent the escape of any
Water. — Any number of such Machines may be used
one below the other as the fall will allow, which at this place
generally used for washing the Ore will allow of almost
any number of them if found convenient for the purposes
designed. — And such Machines will be easily moved
from one situation to another. —

# Untitled

There are two lists accompanying the pictures. This one, comprising eighteen titles, is only a very partial list of some of the illustrations in the two stitched volumes. It is composed in the handwriting of the pencil titles on a few of the drawings. The author of this list is, of course, unknown, and the list is very incomplete. None of the pictures illustrative of ore and lead carriage are here, and only one picture showing the life of miners outside their working environment is on the list. This picture is 'How is the', replacing 'Wrestling' which has been struck through. It seems as though illustrating the processes of mining and ore separation was the key to the compilation of this list. It is interesting to see the title 'Trunking' here. 'Trunking' does not appear on the second, more substantial, index, and there is no extant illustration of trunking in the collection. 'Trunking' is an important stage in the process of ore separation, so one would expect it to be illustrated. Mulcaster[12] showed a trunk buddle (see page 12) and described the process. For those interested in the detail his description is available on the Dukesfield Smelters and Carriers website (www.dukesfield.org.uk).

*Reference number 1985 2032 53. Pencil*

✓ Buddleing 1
✓ Tubbing
  Trunking
✓ Shaddering
✓ Knocking } 2
✓ Grateing } 2
✗ Orguiing
✗ Waggon
✓ Barrow 6
✓ Monday morning 4
✓ Brake — } 3
✓ Going to work
✓ Weighing On & filling 5
✓ Wedge

✓ Blasting
✓ Drawing
✓ Hustling
  Now is the

# Sketches Illustrative [...] Miners

A much more substantial index than the previous list, this one is in the same hand as the inked titles on the pictures, apart from the faint pencil heading in a different hand. This heading is difficult to read and it is not possible to make out all the words. The fact that the numbers refer to 'pages' suggests a serious attempt to catalogue and paginate the pictures in the volumes. However the list is incomplete.

Some of the pictures which carry numbers have not been included in the list, and some of the pictures which are included have not been numbered. The list starts roughly in alphabetical order with B's followed by C's, but then the order becomes completely random. Two items – 'Crack' and 'Poaching' – are added in faint pencil, in a different hand, at the bottom.

So, this unique collection of paintings and drawings ends as it began: enchanting, informative, enigmatic, tantalising, jumbled, unfinished, full of unanswered questions. But its importance as a record of lead mining in the North Pennines during the Regency period is beyond all doubt.

*Reference number 1985 2032 51. Ink with pencil.*

# Notes

1   Phillips Son and Neale London book sale 25,759 lot 532.

2   *An Account of the Mining Districts of Alston Moor, Weardale and Teesdale etc.* Thomas Sopwith, 1833.

3   There is a rather elegant extension on the left-hand side of the current Inn with a weathervane dated 1790 above its roof. This extension is not shown in the drawings. But the weathervane is misleading. It was probably originally on the main house and the extension is not eighteenth, but nineteenth, century in date.

4   Northumberland Record Office 672 E 1E 6.

5   *A Treatise on a Section of the Strata commencing near Newcastle upon Tyne and concluding on the west side of the Mountain of Cross-Fell with remarks on Mineral Veins in General, and Engraved Figures of Some of the different species of these Productions. To which are added Tables of the Strata in Yorkshire and Derbyshire. The whole intended to amuse the Mineralogist and assist the Miner in his Professional Researches*, Westgarth Forster, Second edition, 1821.

6   Hall's reference for the quotation from Bewick is *A Memoir of Thomas Bewick, Written by Himself*, ed. Iain Bain, Oxford University Press, 1975.

7   Reproduced in *Grouse Shooting Made Quite Easy*, ed. Grayling 1998 edition.

8   Detail from page 27 of *Grouse Shooting Made Quite Easy*, ed. Grayling 1998 edition.

9   *Weardale Men and Manners*, J R Featherstone, 1840.

10  *Horse Whims and Gins – A Study*, Gill, Knapp and Gallagher, in *British Mining* N° 98, Memoirs 2014.

11  *A Treatise on a Section of Strata etc.*, Westgarth Forster.

12  *An Accot. of the method of smelting &c. Lead Ore, as it is practised in the Northern part of England, containing an explanation of the several Processes the Ore undergoes, from the time of its being brought to the Mill, to that of its being finaly manufactured into saleable Lead & Bullion there; Together with some accot. of the mode of washing Lead Ore so as to make it fit for Smelting, and a description of those Substances , mineral & fossil, with which the Lead Ore in Alston Moor is generaly accompanied, & the Effects they have upon it in Smelting*, James Mulcaster, 1794.

13  All four of Allan's pictures can be viewed online at https://www.nationalgalleries.org/collection/artists-a-z/a/artist/david-allan/object/lead-processing-at-leadhills-smelting-the-ore-ng-2836.

14  Durham County Record Office D/X 1035/7.

15  Northumberland Record Office 672/A/31/38.

16  *Notes on Allendale,* B. Irwin, 1880.

17  William Morley Egglestone c.1873, paper in author's possession.

# Acknowledgements and further information

This book has been produced as part of the Dukesfield Smelters and Carriers Project (2012 – 2015).

The publication was made possible because the Science and Society Picture Library granted a licence to reproduce the images. We are grateful to the Library for this support. The Scottish National Portrait Gallery granted permission to reproduce the painting on page 14 and the Literary and Philosophical Society of Newcastle-upon-Tyne gave permission to reproduce the images on pages 12 and 21. Newcastle City Library granted permission to reproduce the plate on page 23.

The Dukesfield Smelters and Carriers Project was led by the Friends of the North Pennines and was a partnership between the Friends of the North Pennines and the Parish Councils of Hexhamshire and Slaley. Full details of the project are at www.dukesfield.org.uk, where there is also much more information about lead mining and lead carriage, including a map of the main lead carriage routes to Tyneside.

A very large number of historical documents about the lead mining industry of the North Pennines was transcribed and uploaded to the internet during the project and these Dukesfield Documents form a highly valuable resource for research at www.dukesfield.org.uk/research/dukesfield-documents.

James Mulcaster's complete paper on lead smelting (1794), extracts from which are included in this book, is amongst the wealth of historical material to be found in Dukesfield Documents.

For those who want to read more on the subject of lead mining in the North Pennines, the Background and Support section of Dukesfield Documents contains a very useful bibliography.

Dukesfield Smelters and Carriers was funded by the Heritage Lottery Fund, with additional funding from the HB Allen Charitable Trust, Joicey Trust, Barbour Foundation, Northumberland County Council: Community Chest, Members' Small Schemes (Councillor Colin Horncastle), Sir James Knott Trust, Hexham Local History Society and the Henry Bell Trust.

Many people have helped with the production of this book. The late Arthur Roberts first enthused me about the pictures many years ago. Margaret and Alec Manchester tracked down the information about Jacob Dawson and his inn at Allenheads. Greg Finch read and advised on the draft text. Pam Forbes provided advice and endless encouragement. I am grateful to all of them: they have improved the book. The remaining errors are mine alone.